CIVIL WAR
MYTHS & LEGENDS

THE TRUE STORIES BEHIND
HISTORY'S MYSTERIES

SECOND EDITION

MICHAEL R. BRADLEY

Globe
Pequot

Guilford, Connecticut

Globe
Pequot

An imprint of The Rowman & Littlefield Publishing Group, Inc.
4501 Forbes Blvd., Ste. 200
Lanham, MD 20706
www.rowman.com

Distributed by NATIONAL BOOK NETWORK

British Library Cataloguing in Publication Information available

Library of Congress Cataloging-in-Publication Data available

ISBN 978-1-4930-3976-0 (paperback)
ISBN 978-1-4930-3977-7 (e-book)

♾™ The paper used in this publication meets the minimum requirements of American National Standard for Information Sciences—Permanence of Paper for Printed Library Materials, ANSI/NISO Z39.48-1992

Printed in the United States of America

CONTENTS

CONTENTS

PREFACE

The Civil War of 1861–65 is indeed the stuff of which mysteries and legends are made. The record of the war has been called "the American Iliad." Across the South, in New England, through the Midwest, and even on the West Coast, there are buildings and locations that are the locus of oft-retold stories associated with the Civil War. Many of these accounts have taken on the aura of legends, while other aspects of the conflict and its memory have been cloaked in mystery.

While the war has inspired a massive amount of fiction writing over the past century and a half, there is no need for a writer to create imaginary tales of ghosts and mysterious events concerning the war. The history of the conflict, and the memories that are a part of that history, provide a plethora of factual material with which to work.

Some of the legends swirling around the Civil War and its participants represent a skewing of facts, something that always seems to happen when stories are told and retold across generations. After all, as one of my grandfathers told me when I was a boy, "Every story deserves to be a little better than it really was." Thus, Stonewall Jackson's love of fresh fruit becomes an obsessive sucking on lemons; Ulysses Grant's occasional enjoyment of a drink or two becomes a story of debauched alcoholism. The confusion and chaos at the end of the war as the Confederate government shatters and fragments produces mysterious stories of enormous hoards of gold and treasure hidden in multiple locations. Such stories have a kernel of truth even though they have become the basis for legends.

Instead of collecting quaint stories of ghosts and mysterious events, the purpose of this book is to look at the facts behind some of the mysteries and legends from the Civil War and to put them in a proper factual and historical setting. These stories retain their fascinating character even when they are stripped of the elements that make them "a little better than they really were."

The Civil War changed the United States in many ways—politically, socially, and economically. No wonder that mysteries and legends came to surround it. No wonder that more than a century and a half later the stories of that conflict still engage us. It behooves us all to look at those turbulent times and, from those days, draw courage and insight to assist us in dealing with the challenges of our times.

CHAPTER 1

Words-War-Wilderness

The *Oxford English Dictionary* (OED) is universally acclaimed as the absolute authority on the meaning, pronunciation, and development of more than 500,000 words in the English language. In giving the history and meanings of words, the OED uses two and a half million quotations that contributors submit from sources ranging from history and classical literature to motion picture scripts. The entire text of the twenty-volume print edition contains approximately fifty-nine million words. The beginnings of the OED can be traced to members of the Philological Society of Great Britain in 1857. Their efforts would not produce a first print edition until 1928.

As the OED was being developed, the Civil War was raging in the United States. This military conflict would find a connection with the massive scholarly undertaking going on in Britain. Specifically, there would be a connection between the 1864 Battle of the Wilderness and the OED, a strange and mysterious connection not made widely known until more than 130 years later.

The connection begins on the far side of the earth from both the United States and Great Britain, and it involves the child of a missionary couple. William Chester Minor came from a highly respectable background. He was born in the country then called Ceylon, now known as Sri Lanka, in 1834. His father had gone to that nation as a missionary of the Congregational Church. This church has its roots in New England and traces its development to the Puritan settlers of the seventeenth century. William was tutored by his father until the age of fourteen, at which time he was sent to the United States to continue his education. An uncle lived in New Haven, Connecticut, and the schools there welcomed the young man.

By 1848 sectional tensions were rising in the United States and William arrived in Connecticut as the debate over what would become known as "the compromise of 1850" was beginning. At the time there were equal numbers of slave-holding states and free states. Since each state had two senators, this balance created a tie on anti-slavery votes in the Senate, which meant no anti-slavery legislation could pass. The 1849 Gold Rush brought hordes of people to California, and what had been, legally, only a territory now wanted to become a state. The admission of California to the Union would break the deadlock between free and slave states, and the debate over what to do caused great political stress before it was agreed that California could be admitted as a free state but that no anti-slavery legislation would be considered by Congress. Clearly, this agreement did not satisfy extreme groups on either side. The debate over slavery and states' rights would continue.

It took William six years to complete his pre-collegiate and collegiate studies. At age twenty he entered the Yale University

Medical Department and then spent time as an apprentice to a practicing doctor. By 1863 William C. Minor was an accomplished physician with a sterling reputation and a bright future in his chosen profession. The Civil War was at its bloody height, and the army needed all the doctors it could find. Following the call of his country and the desire to learn more about medicine, Dr. Minor became a "contract surgeon."

The United States Army did not have a fully developed medical corps at the time of the Civil War. The army contracted with civilian doctors, or "contract surgeons," to provide medical care for soldiers. These surgeons were given a nominal rank, usually captain for new hires or major for more experienced men, and this rank allowed the doctors to be paid and to draw rations from the army commissary. Musicians usually did duty as stretcher bearers, although many wounded men were brought to the field hospitals by friends. During a battle there was usually no shortage of men ready to leave the firing line to help a wounded comrade to the rear. In the field hospitals there would be a small staff of assistants to perform nursing duties, although this staff generally had only sketchy, on-the-job training. Civilian volunteers were often present and were much appreciated.

By contemporary standards, the medical practices of Civil War doctors seem quite crude. Surgical instruments were not sterilized, because there was no perceived need to do so, nor were means of sterilization readily available. Dressings on wounds were changed irregularly, and the same bandages were replaced on the wound once it had been inspected. Bullets that had lodged in a person's body were located by probing the wound with a metal rod or, on occasion, with a finger. Obviously, infection was a constant threat and there was little available in the way of treatment. Contagious diseases were more deadly than bullets, and doctors had no drugs to combat the most common of illnesses.

However, Civil War medicine was not simple butchery. Folk tales to the contrary, most surgery was done under anesthesia, thereby lessening the shock to the system of the wounded man. Only rarely did field hospitals run short of chloroform. Actually, the presence of chloroform was sometimes a problem for doctors. The sleep-inducing liquid was administered to a patient by placing a wire-mesh cone (covered with a cloth) over the nose and mouth, then pouring a small quantity of the liquid over the cone. The surgeon standing over patients for hours on end would breathe these fumes over a long period of time, often becoming very sleepy or nauseated as a result. Many doctors smoked cigars while operating just to avoid the odor of chloroform.

It is true that Dr. Minor would have performed large numbers of amputations. This had as much to do with military technology as it did with medical science. By 1863 the majority of soldiers, Union and Confederate, were armed with rifles, usually .59-caliber Springfields or .57-caliber Enfields. These weapons were accurate to 300 yards and more, though the soldiers seldom fired at extreme ranges. Despite their accuracy, the weapons had a relatively low muzzle velocity, meaning the impact of the rifle slug was not as great as it might have been. Further, the weapons fired a bullet of soft lead. When this low-velocity missile struck a human body, the slug penetrated, mushroomed, and did not go out the other side. The bullet stayed in the wound along with shreds of cloth from the soldier's uniform.

If the soft-lead bullet struck a bone, the impact caused extensive splintering of the bone above and below the point of impact. The most effective treatment available was to amputate the limb above the area of splintering. However, the amputation was done under anesthesia, and post-operative painkillers were available in the form of laudanum, a potent drug consisting of heroin powder dissolved in alcohol. This was an effective, though addictive, painkiller.

Despite the horrifying accounts of piles of severed arms and legs outside field hospitals, most amputees survived the operation. Infection was the big killer, and neither Dr. Minor nor any other physician had a treatment for that. Much depended on the rude good health and resilience of the patient.

Serving first in an army hospital in New Haven, Dr. Minor had a gentle introduction to Civil War combat and the treatment of wounds. Although he had signed up with the army just days before the Battle of Gettysburg, Dr. Minor was far from the battlefield. A soldier evacuated from Gettysburg who reached New Haven was likely to recover. He might have awful scars from wounds, but the soldier had an excellent chance of going home.

In the spring of 1864, under the supervision of General Ulysses S. Grant, the armies of the United States went on a coordinated offensive. General William T. Sherman was on the offensive in Georgia while Grant kept a personal eye on the Army of the Potomac, commanded by General George Meade, in Virginia. The pressure on the Confederacy would be great, the casualties would be tremendous. Dr. Minor was called up to the front line.

On May 4, 1864, the Union Army of the Potomac crossed the Rapidan River and moved south. The roads they were following passed through a seventy-square-mile tangle of second-growth timber, brush, and vines called "The Wilderness." The Confederate Army of Northern Virginia quickly moved into this wooded area to offer battle. The thick tangle of vegetation would make cavalry and artillery almost useless, so the fight would be an infantryman's battle. The outnumbered Confederates would have some advantage since the larger Union army could not be fully deployed in the heavy timber. The terrain also meant the fighting would be at very close range; often visibility was limited to twenty yards or so.

For three days the soldiers on both sides blasted away at each other, or at where each thought the other might be. By the second day the woods had caught fire, filling the air with smoke and burning to death many wounded men who could not get out of the way. Although the phrase had not become a part of Civil War parlance, Dr. Minor learned that "war is hell."

On May 8 both armies moved south and east a few miles and a degree of peace came to The Wilderness. The frantic pace of performing triage, of treating wounds, of amputating limbs slowly slackened. Dr. Minor found himself shaken to the foundation of his soul. But a fresh horror awaited him. A soldier, an Irish immigrant, had been arrested for desertion, brought to trial, and found guilty.

The Civil War was often said to be "a rich man's war and a poor man's fight." While both South and North had a military draft, the laws allowed a draftee to hire a substitute to go fight in his place. In the North, many immigrants who could not find jobs signed up as substitutes to take the place of draftees. Obviously, such men had little motivation to be good soldiers and many of them deserted. The Articles of War called for deserters to be shot to death, but there was a provision for "other lesser punishment." This "lesser punishment" was branding on both cheeks with the letter "D."

When corporal punishment was to be administered, it was done publicly, usually in the presence of the culprit's comrades in arms, and the punishment was administered by a noncommissioned officer. In the situation of this particular Irish immigrant, for some unknown reason Dr. Minor was ordered to inflict the punishment. Perhaps Minor was not considered "an officer and a gentleman" since he was a civilian under contract. Perhaps the officer commanding the unit wanted to avoid friction within his ranks by having an outsider inflict the punishment. At any rate, Dr. Minor did the deed; he held the glowing hot iron to the face of the Irish soldier while the man screamed and thrashed against his restraints. The memory of that terrible moment never left Dr. Minor's mind; it ate its way into his psyche. Slowly, Dr. Minor's mind wandered into its own Wilderness, where it would fight a different kind of battle.

As soon as the field hospitals could be cleared of men well enough to travel, long lines of ambulances left the battlefield heading for Fredericksburg, Virginia, where the wounded men were placed on steamboats for the journey by water to Washington, DC. Dr. Minor accompanied some of these men and was assigned to a hospital in the nation's capital for the remainder of the war. His work was highly thought of by those who supervised him, and he maintained a lively interest in learning all he could about his profession. Clearly, the presence of so many wounded men helped doctors develop new methods of treatment and consider new theories of practicing medicine.

Despite the horrors he had seen and the act he had been ordered to perform on the deserter, Dr. Minor felt at home in the army. He sought to become more than a civilian under contract; he wanted to join the select ranks of men commissioned to serve in the Medical Corps. By the time the war ended in 1865, he had achieved this goal and was a captain in the regular army of the United States.

The first postwar assignment Dr. Minor received was to an army post in New York City, a choice posting. But something was happening to the physician, something he could not heal himself. His mind took a strange turn; he could not sleep and so walked the streets until the small hours of the morning. He developed what today would be called "sexual addiction" and spent a great deal of time in the company of prostitutes. The quality of his medical work declined, and he became quite apprehensive when in the company of Irish people. This was a problem in New York because the city was filled with Irishmen, both long-term residents and newcomers arriving daily.

Disappointed with someone who had been a rising star, and hoping to help him, the army assigned Dr. Minor to Pensacola, Florida. The boredom of this isolated post and the very hot weather of the summer season only made the matter worse. Dr. Minor's symptoms of mental distress became more obvious, and it was decided that the ailing physician should be sent to the asylum now called St. Elizabeth's in Washington, DC.

The asylum was a rather pleasant place in a rural setting. Famous people, including Abraham Lincoln, used it as a weekend retreat from the city. As a nonviolent patient, Dr. Minor lived in a small apartment and could come and go as he pleased, regularly going into town to draw his pay at the War Department or to shop. From time to time, however, he was subject to episodes of strong delusions and to unreasoning fears.

By 1870 Dr. Minor had been placed on the army's "retired list"—in modern terms, he was given an honorable discharge since his disability was deemed to be service-related. Could this be a case of what is today called post-traumatic stress disorder? In 1871 Minor moved to London, hoping a change of scenery would prove beneficial. It did not.

Not only did Dr. Minor return to his old dissolute way of life, he was surrounded by strangers and this fed his apprehensions, fears, and delusions. Minor had brought a pistol with him from the United States, and he began to go out armed at all times. The doctor was especially concerned about his forced association with the crowds of Irishmen found on the streets of London. On February 17, 1872, something snapped. Late that night, while restlessly roaming the streets, Minor shot and killed one George Merrit. Minor would tell the police he feared that Merrit was about to attack and rob him; actually, Merrit was a peaceful man with a large family who was on his way to work.

At the trial there was extensive testimony about Dr. Minor's past, including his mental condition. At the conclusion of the proceedings the jury brought in a verdict of "not guilty, by reason that the balance of his mind was deranged." Saved from the noose, Dr. Minor was sent to the Broadmoor Criminal Lunatic Asylum at Crowthorne, to stay "at Her Majesty's pleasure."

At the same time as Dr. Minor was being sent to Broadmoor, James Murray was becoming the editor for the long-discussed, slowly developing project that would become the OED. Looking for much-needed help who would work for free, Murray placed ads in newspapers and distributed flyers through booksellers asking readers to report as many quotations as they could for ordinary English words. He also asked for quotes dealing with unusual words, either old or new. These quotations should be submitted to Murray as soon as he published a list of terms for which he needed illustrative quotes.

In the Broadmoor Asylum, Dr. Minor had a range of privileges open to him, since he was not considered a danger to himself or to others so long as he was observed regularly. He had a small suite of rooms in which he could pursue a favorite pastime, painting, and where he could house his library. Since he still drew his army retirement, Dr. Minor purchased newspapers and books by mail. Perhaps this is how he learned of Murray's project. At any rate, the doctor opened a correspondence with the editor of the OED.

As Murray sent out lists of the words for which he wanted quotations, Dr. Minor read through his ever-growing library and set up a card file of words and the quotes that illustrated their various meanings. Soon, as quickly as Murray published a new list, a package would arrive from Crowthorne with dozens of slips of paper containing well-chosen quotes illustrating the use of the words. Minor became one of the most dependable and productive contributors to the project; indeed, he was a prolific writer. It

Murray frequently wrote to Minor thanking him for his work and asking if they could meet. However, Murray found it impossible to get away from his editorial work and Minor always sent a reasonable excuse for his inability to travel to Oxford to meet the editor. So it remained for twenty years. At last there came a time when Murray could be away for a few days. He wrote to Minor to say he was coming to visit and, by return mail, received an address to which he should come when he arrived in Crowthorne.

When the train pulled into the station, the editor asked directions and soon was standing in front of an imposing house. When the door opened to his knock, he was shown into a room lined floor to ceiling with books, but the man behind the desk was not Dr. Minor; it was the warden of the asylum. For the first time, Murray learned that the best contributor to the OED was, by law, criminally insane.

Sadly, the mind of Dr. Minor went deeper and deeper into his mental Wilderness. At last he was allowed to return to the United States to an asylum near his family. The developing science of psychoanalysis identified his illness as schizophrenia. The unfortunate, but literate, doctor died in 1920.

Today scholars, students, and curious people all over the world consult the *Oxford English Dictionary* in print or in its online version. It is still the final authority on the usage and meaning of English words. But, how many of these people are aware of the mysterious connection between its words and the Civil War—in particular, the Battle of the Wilderness?

CHAPTER 2

The Yankee Behind Nathan Bedford Forrest's Saddle

Two days of hard fighting had just come to an end around a little Methodist church whose name, Shiloh, meant "place of peace." For the 23,000 men lying dead or wounded for miles around the modest structure, it was anything but a peaceful place. Now the Confederate army was inching away from the battlefield on its way to Corinth, Mississippi, some twenty miles away, with the US army inching along in pursuit. In command of the Confederate rearguard was a cavalry colonel who had already made something of a reputation for himself. His name was Nathan Bedford Forrest.

On April 8, 1862, Forrest had about 350 men under his command. Men from Mississippi, Texas, and Kentucky held themselves ready to obey any orders issued by the bold Tennessee leader. For two days these cavalrymen had watched the infantry and artillery slug it out and now they were ready to get personally involved. Forrest had arrived on the field at Shiloh as the colonel commanding the Third Tennessee Cavalry Regiment. He had spent the two days of the battle seeking a place where his mounted men could be used effectively, but the wooded terrain of the battlefield offered him little opportunity for action. When the Confederate retreat began, Forrest's regiment was assigned to its second-in-command and Forrest was selected to command the rear-guard.

Forrest had found a good spot to fight a rear-guard action. The road he was protecting came down a long cleared slope and crossed a sluggish stream with swampy, muddy bands. Timber had been cut along the stream during the drier months, and the now-marshy area was littered with tree tops, brush, and some logs. The ground rose after crossing the stream and went up a wooded slope and over a crest. Forrest posted his men in a line over the crest, out of the sight of pursuers.

General William T. Sherman led the advance for the US Army with two brigades of infantry and the Fourth Illinois Cavalry. Using standard military tactics of the day, Sherman had some infantry skirmishers out front followed by the cavalry and the bulk of his infantry marching along the road in a compact formation.

Forrest waited until Sherman's skirmishers were in the slow process of crossing the swampy creek. Then the Southern horsemen moved quietly down the slope and suddenly burst out of the trees screaming the Rebel yell. Most of the cavalrymen were armed with double-barrel shotguns and many also carried a revolver. At a range of twenty yards, the shotguns were an effective and deadly weapon. Surprised, and their ranks riddled with buckshot, the skirmishers threw down their rifles and ran. The Fourth Illinois Cavalry, now facing the screeching, pistol-waving Confederates, did the same, fleeing as fast as their horses could splash through the mud and water.

This was the time for Forrest to stop the attack and to fall back. The enemy pursuit had been checked, and there were far too many Yankees in Sherman's main infantry column for a handful of cavalry to attack. Following this sound principle of military doctrine, most of the cavalry held back. For some reason, Forrest did not.

Forrest was known to "get his blood up" when in a fight. Although he was described as usually calm and mild in manner when in combat, one close associate said that "his face glowed like heated bronze and his eyes glared like a panther." Perhaps that is what happened. Or perhaps Forrest was so fixed on the men in his immediate front who were running that he never noticed the steady blue lines beyond them. At any rate, Forrest kept galloping ahead and soon was surrounded by men who were firing at him from all sides. One opponent placed the muzzle of his rifle against Forrest's left hip and pulled the trigger. The .59-caliber soft-lead slug ripped through Forrest's flesh and lodged near his spine. The impact of the slug lifted him free of the saddle and left his right leg numb.

Yelling, firing his revolver, and clubbing men with the weapon when it was empty, Forrest broke free of the ring of enemies and, as he dashed back toward his own lines, seized a Yankee soldier by the coat collar, swung this human shield onto the horse's back behind the saddle, and rode away sheltered by his unwilling human bulwark.

Or so says the story.

Nathan Bedford Forrest was a big man, physically. He stood well over six feet in height and weighed about 170 pounds, this at a time when the average American male was about five feet seven inches in height, weighed about 135 pounds, and had a thirty-six-inch chest when he inhaled. Physically, Forrest stood out in a crowd. He had grown up on farms in Tennessee and Mississippi, and a vigorous outdoor life had made him a muscular adult. By April 1862 he had been in the military service for a year, and this active duty had given him a hearty and healthy constitution despite his age of forty-one. But, even so, could Forrest reach out with his right hand, grab a US soldier by the collar, and swing the unwilling captive up behind him on his horse?

Forrest's right leg was numb from the impact of the bullet against his spine, so he could not brace himself with that leg in the stirrup to gain leverage. The colonel would definitely have used his right hand for this purpose since he was naturally left-handed and would have been using his pistol with that hand. Also, the angle of Forrest's grip on the captive's coat collar makes it almost impossible for him to have set the man behind him, even had he been able to swing the captive to that height; an unwounded man with both feet in the stirrups might have been able to swing a person up in front of him, but not behind.

Why was this legend created, and why has it persisted?

Forrest was already a legendary figure by the time he fought the rear-guard action after the Battle of Shiloh. When the war began he was a wealthy businessman in Memphis. He openly opposed secession and voted against Tennessee leaving the Union when the first vote on secession was taken in February 1861. Most Tennesseans agreed with Forrest, and the state remained in the Union until shots were fired at Fort Sumter in April 1861 and Lincoln called for 75,000 volunteers to put down what the president called "a domestic insurrection." Now that a war had begun the only question for Forrest, and for Tennessee, was which side to join. A second vote on secession was taken in June 1861 and, this time, the vote was heavily in favor of leaving the Union. Immediately, Forrest joined the forces being raised by the state of Tennessee and enlisted as a private.

Within a few weeks Forrest had been asked to raise a battalion of cavalry and was given the rank of lieutenant colonel. By October 1861 he had his command recruited, organized, trained, and armed. To accomplish the latter task Forrest did not depend on the slender resources of Tennessee or the Confederacy. He dressed in civilian clothing, traveled by train to Louisville, Kentucky, and used his own money to purchase weapons for his men. These guns were then hidden in wagons under loads of innocent-seeming cargo such as hay or oats, and the wagons were driven south by men from Kentucky who wanted to join the Confederate forces.

Before Christmas 1861 Forrest had led his men to the banks of the Ohio River and had won his first victory in an engagement at Sacramento, Kentucky. In his first battle Forrest insisted on leading from the front, calling on his men to follow him instead of sending them into danger while he stayed in the rear. His exploits took on "star power" in February 1862. A large force of infantry, protected by a new weapon of warfare—armored gunboats—had traveled by riverboats up the Tennessee River to attack a Confederate position at Fort Henry. The flooding river had driven the Rebel garrison out of the fort, so the US troops, commanded by General Ulysses Grant, won an easy victory. Grant then marched his men across a narrow neck of land to attack Fort Donelson, which guarded the Cumberland River.

Forrest and his cavalry were part of the garrison at Fort Donelson. Fulfilling the proper role for cavalry, Forrest and his command delayed Grant's march across the peninsula as much as they were able and then participated in two days of heavy combat in an attempt to force the Union army back to the Tennessee River. When this attempt failed, the Confederate high command began to discuss surrender. Learning of this, Forrest let it be known in no uncertain terms that he had no intention of surrendering. On the night before the capitulation was to take place, Forrest led his command, and any others who dared join him, across a freezing backwater of the Cumberland River and marched them off to Nashville, almost a hundred miles away. Forrest and his 1,000 followers escaped while 14,000 stayed behind to surrender.

Panic was loose in the streets of Nashville when the news arrived that Fort Donelson had surrendered. Nothing stood between the gunboats of the US Navy and the city, but Forrest took charge, keeping order in the streets and overseeing the evacuation of tons of food supplies and military material.

So began a long career for Forrest, a career marked by bold, decisive action. As the Union forces occupied Middle Tennessee in the summer following the Battle of Shiloh, Forrest led a raid on the railroad town of Murfreesboro. This attack, made on his birthday, July 13, 1862, won him promotion to brigadier general. It also led to the Union advance on Chattanooga being stopped in order to pay attention to protecting the supply line that supported the advance. This pause allowed the Confederates to move their army into Kentucky, effectively nullifying much of the progress the Union had made in the West in the first year of the war.

By December 1862 one US army under Grant was threatening Vicksburg, Mississippi, while another US army under William S. Rosecrans had made its way back into Middle Tennessee and was again threatening to move toward the vital railroad junction of Chattanooga. Faced with these threats, Forrest led 1,200 men across the Tennessee River on a raid lasting two weeks. This raid so effectively damaged the railroads leading south as to create a serious shortage of supplies among Union troops, stopping the advance of both Grant and Rosecrans for the next six months. In addition to the strategic importance of this raid, Forrest improved the fighting ability of his own command. He took 1,200 men into the raid and brought 2,200 out of it, having recruited an additional 1,000 men. At the beginning of the movement, his men were insufficiently armed, many carrying shotguns. At the end of the raid, his men carried the best weapons the US government could offer, having captured enough arms to reequip themselves.

In April 1863 Union Colonel Abel Streight took a brigade of men mounted on mules across the mountainous terrain of North Alabama in an attempt to reach and destroy a vital railroad that ran from Atlanta to Chattanooga. Forrest found out about the move more than twenty-four hours after Streight had acted, but he pursued and caught the raiders. Pinning them down near Gaylesville, Alabama, Forrest sent in a message demanding their surrender. While his demand was being considered, he had his men and artillery march around hills and across openings in the woods so the Yankees would count them again and again. Convinced he was badly outnumbered, Streight surrendered his command to a force less than half his own.

At the Battle of Chickamauga in September 1863, Forrest led his men into the thick of the battle, dismounting them to fight as infantry. His cavalrymen performed so well that General Daniel H. Hill commented that they were such skillful fighters on foot that he did not know they were cavalry until he saw the yellow trim on their uniforms identifying their branch of service.

Shortly after that battle, Forrest had a confrontation with Braxton Bragg, the commander of the Confederate army. Forrest was disgusted with Bragg's inability to capture the Union army now trapped in Chattanooga, and he expressed his feelings in an unrestrained fashion. According to an eyewitness, Forrest cursed his superior officer and told him "if you were any part of a man I would slap your jaws and force you to resent it." Forrest meant he was ready to challenge Bragg to a duel, but he knew Bragg did not have the personal courage to accept a challenge. Of course, such acts were a violation of military law and Forrest could have been arrested and court-martialed, but he knew that would not happen either. The Forrest legend would not permit it.

Shortly after this confrontation, Forrest was transferred to northern Mississippi and placed in charge of defending an area that provided huge amounts of critical food supplies for the Southern cause. Forrest arrived in Mississippi accompanied only by his personal escort of some hundred men *and* a single battery of artillery. He called on the scattered groups of Confederates active in the area and organized them into regiments. Then he penetrated into West Tennessee to recruit men and to capture the weapons needed to arm them. Time after time expeditions were sent against Forrest, and each time the attacks were stopped, with Forrest defeating each expedition even though he was consistently outnumbered. On one occasion Forrest led a small group of raiders into the Union headquarters in Memphis and caused the commanding general to flee in his nightshirt to avoid capture.

It was during this time that a dark shadow was added to Forrest's reputation. In April 1864 men under his command raided into West Tennessee, reaching the banks of the Ohio River at Paducah, Kentucky. As part of this raid Forrest sent some of his men to attack the US position at Fort Pillow, a fortified post on the Mississippi River. The garrison of the fort was composed of Tennessee Unionists and African Americans recruited from Tennessee. Local residents had made complaints against the garrison, saying that the men there did not respect private property and their behavior toward women was improper.

The fighting at the fort ended when Forrest's men made a frontal assault that took them over the breastworks, into the fort. A large percentage of the garrison became a casualty of battle. A Congressional Investigating Committee charged that many men, especially African Americans, had been killed after surrendering. Forrest denied that men had been killed after surrendering and pointed out that the garrison had been given two chances to surrender and had refused both of them. Indeed, the US flag was still flying when his men stormed the breastworks, and it was Confederates who lowered the flag to indicate that the action should come to an end.

The incident at Fort Pillow was much discussed in the North, and it was used by the Republican Party to stir up support for the war at a time when many were longing for peace; indeed, Lincoln was fearful of not being reelected the following November, so the charges may have had some political motivation behind them. There can be no doubt, however, that unjustified deaths did occur at Fort Pillow. At any rate, no action, during or after the war, was taken against Forrest, but the legendary nature of the man became more complex, more tinged with controversy.

Forrest was such an efficient fighter that General Sherman, from 1864 onward the commander of all US troops in the Western theater, said that he had to be stopped even if it cost the lives of 10,000 Union soldiers and bankrupted the government. On another occasion Sherman referred to "that devil Forrest." During the campaign that ended with the capture of Atlanta, Sherman had more concern for Forrest in his rear, threatening his line of supplies, than he had for the Confederate army confronting him. Faced with yet another of Forrest's numerous raids into Union-held territory, Sherman fumed, "There will never be peace in Tennessee so long as Forrest lives." Even to his enemies Forrest was a legend. Even in his own lifetime, extraordinary stories clustered around him.

During the course of the war, Forrest killed twenty-nine men in personal combat and had thirty horses killed under him. Beginning as a private, he surrendered with the rank of lieutenant general. During the war he commanded troops from nine of the thirteen Confederate states. Those who served under his leadership tended to respond with fierce loyalty and deep devotion. Many an old "Johnny Reb" proudly boasted for the rest of their lives that "I rode with Forrest."

So why the unlikely story of the Union soldier caught up as a shield in the rear-guard action after Shiloh? In the eyes of many of his contemporaries, and in the eyes of many Civil War students, Forrest was and is larger than life. However, no Confederate veteran writing during or after the war ever claimed to be an eyewitness to this particular feat. No Union soldier ever stepped forward to say that he was the man so used. The first account of Forrest's military career, *The Campaigns of General Nathan Bedford Forrest,* was published in 1868 when the general was alive. It is thought by many historians that Forrest read and approved the manuscript for this work, and in its pages there is no mention of swooping up a Union soldier from the ground and using him as a shield.

John Allan Wyeth, a former Confederate cavalryman who became one of the leading surgeons in the United States, wrote a biography of Forrest based, in large part, on interviews and correspondence with men who fought under Forrest as well as with those who fought against him. This book, today published under the title *That Devil Forrest,* makes no mention of the incident. William Forrest, Nathan's son, lived a long life and frequently spoke at meetings of old veterans. William never told this story. Still, despite a lack of all historical evidence, the story continues to be told. It seems that men who are larger than life in deed and reputation are often credited for deeds that border on the impossible. Legendary men create legends.

CHAPTER 3

Ulysses S. Grant: The Perpetual Drunk?

"Grant, of course, was drunk." This statement was made uncounted times in personal letters, in conversations private and public, and in print during and after the Civil War. Actually, the comment first appeared long before the war. Ulysses S. Grant is branded in the pages of much of Civil War history as a drunk—indeed, as a perpetual drunk. The accounts of his prodigious drinking habits reached the White House on more than one occasion and were said to have led Lincoln to comment, "What brand of whiskey does he drink? I would like to send a barrel of it to my other generals to see if it would make them fight."

According to many accounts, Grant drank heavily while serving in the war with Mexico; was habitually drunk while assigned to duty in California in the 1850s, so much so that he resigned his commission one step ahead of a court-martial; could not find a civilian job because of his drinking; and was rescued from the gutter by his father. When the Civil War began, Grant tried to shake off his old ways but found the boredom of much of army life and the ready presence of liquor too tempting, so he soused himself in the bottle again. Charges flew that Grant was drunk for several days, allowing his army to be surprised at Shiloh, and he was said to have been on a three-day binge during the Vicksburg Campaign. The general found solace in drink during the dull days after the fall of Vicksburg, and he had to be closely watched during the 1864–65 campaign in Virginia to ensure that all liquor was kept away from him or that his indulgence wasn't seen by the army and the general public.

Grant, it was often said, never met a bottle he didn't like, to the extent that some of his associates called him "Useless" Grant. These allegations about him persisted beyond the war years and followed him into the White House and until the end of his life. While on his post-presidential "Grand Tour" of Europe, Grant is said to have made alcohol-inspired overtures to a female member of the British royal family. Queen Victoria, needless to say, was "not amused."

For several weeks prior to the Battle of Shiloh in April 1862, Grant had made his headquarters in a mansion belonging to the Cherry family of Savannah, Tennessee. Mr. Cherry, the owner of the mansion and a prosperous plantation, was a Union supporter despite being a major slave owner. In 1862 he did not see the war as constituting a threat to slavery, so he invited the US commander to make his headquarters in his house. Mrs. Cherry, on the other hand, was strongly pro-Confederate and is said to have eavesdropped on Union planning meetings, smuggling information to Confederate authorities. Shortly after Grant's stay, rumors circulated of wild, alcohol-fueled parties held in the mansion. The fact that attacking

Confederates surprised Grant's army on April 6, 1862, only added credence to the rumors. Grant's defenders are quick to say that the rumors were part of a plot hatched by Mrs. Cherry to discredit Grant, a plot that continues to be examined long after the death of all the participants. Other rumors and allegations are not so easily dismissed.

Grant grew up at a time when the United States was a hard-drinking nation. Distilling fruit into brandy and using grain, especially corn, to make whiskey was a simple and practical solution to turning heavy, perishable commodities into nonperishable, easily transportable goods. As a result, every community had a distillery or "still house." There were no painkillers or stress relievers readily available, so alcohol was accepted as a "cure-all" for physical and psychological issues. Around 1840 public opinion began to change. The discovery and wide distribution of opium-based drugs provided an alternative to alcohol (the twenty-first century knows about the problems of drug addiction; the nineteenth knew about the problems of alcohol). Churches began to oppose the use of alcohol as a beverage, and the Temperance movement began having as its goal the closing of all saloons in the United States. People who drank to excess began to be viewed as morally inferior. Ulysses S. Grant came into manhood as these changes in social opinion were taking place.

During the Mexican War Grant did not have the opportunity to win promotion by leading troops in combat, as was the case with many of his friends and classmates from West Point. Although he served honorably, he received a promotion of only one grade. In 1848 he married Julia Dent. Although the two were devoted to each other, their families each had reservations. The Dents felt their daughter had married beneath herself, and the Grants felt Julia had extravagant tastes.

Only a few years after their marriage, Grant was assigned to duty at Fort Humboldt, an isolated army post in California; it was a posting that did not allow his wife and two children to accompany him. Not only was he separated from his wife and young children, he did not have much to do, since his official duties were light. In this situation Grant became depressed, and alcohol became a problem for him. While no documented evidence has ever been presented of this period in his life, even Grant's closest and most supportive friends thought he was drinking to excess. For some reason, he resigned from the army on April 11, 1854, effective July 31 of that year. Rightly or not, his fellow officers believed that drink was a major cause of his leaving the army.

Grant then entered the most trying period of his life. His father felt that Julia was not an economical housewife, and his father-in-law felt his daughter had taken a step down in marrying Grant. Not fully at ease with either family, Grant took his wife to be near her relatives and tried his hand at farming in Missouri. During this time Grant saved and borrowed enough money to purchase a slave, William Jones, and was given the labor of four other slaves—Eliz, Julia, John, and Dan—who had come to him as the property of his wife. Even with the labor of five slaves, Grant did not make a successful farmer, but the presence of his family and the constant demands on his time and energy kept him clear of the bottle. By 1858 the farm had been sold, the slaves were leased to nearby property owners, and the Grant family started looking for a new home. Eventually that new home was found in Galena, Illinois. In Galena Grant was employed by his father as a clerk in the family leather business.

Neighbors were quite aware of Grant's failures in his earlier careers as a soldier and a farmer, so it is to be expected that a small town's watchful eye followed him in Galena. No one recorded seeing Grant drunk, although it was customary for men to gather at a downtown location after business hours to smoke and gossip after supper. On these occasions a bottle was often present and Grant did not always refuse a social nip.

The Civil War gave a new focus to the life of Ulysses Grant. Now there was important work for which he was qualified, and the demands of that work would keep him busy. Beginning as the drill master for a local group of volunteers, it took only a few weeks for the clerk in the leather store to become a brigadier general.

While in Galena Grant had met a lawyer, John Aaron Rawlins, and the two had become friendly. Rawlins served, at first, as a volunteer aide to Grant but was convinced to join the army. Receiving the rank of captain, Rawlins was appointed to a position on Grant's staff. Rawlins would remain in close company with Grant for the rest of the war. The attorney-turned-staff-officer was a staunch advocate of prohibition and cast a jaundiced eye on all those who drank alcohol. He presumed on his relationship with Grant to make himself the watchdog of Grant's conscience and the monitor of his consumption of alcohol. For Rawlins, even one drop of wine was too much.

By February 1862 Grant was in the national headlines due to his twin victories at Forts Henry and Donelson in Tennessee. With fame and success, however, came jealousy from other officers and renewed rumors about heavy drinking.

After the February victories there ensued a time of refitting, recruiting, and reorganizing for Grant and his army. These routine duties did not keep Grant fully occupied, so this was a time of vulnerability to bad habits. The jealousy of higher-ranking officers caused telegrams to fly from Grant's headquarters to St. Louis, where General Henry Halleck was located, and on to Washington, DC. Halleck was Grant's immediate superior officer and he was very suspicious of Grant's abilities, despite the obvious successes that had been achieved. Halleck seized on a minor infraction of army regulations to have Grant suspended of command and another officer placed over the army while the matter was investigated. Following the bright dawn of victory at Forts Henry and Donelson, Grant's future prospects were gloomy in the days of February and March 1862.

Grant's critics, both those contemporary to him and those of today, argue that he drank heavily during this period. They point to numerous stories told by a variety of people over a wide area. Grant's supporters, then and now, claim that crucial facts are lacking in each case of alleged drunkenness and that there are conflicting stories as to whether or not Grant was drinking. The historical facts are that the investigation of Grant ended and he resumed his command—just in time for the Battle of Shiloh.

The camps of the United States army commanded by Grant sprawled over several miles of flat, wooded terrain upriver (south) of the town of Savannah, Tennessee. Grant was not camped with his troops but was comfortably ensconced in the Cherry mansion in Savannah. There were no field fortifications protecting the camps, and scouting was inadequate, although it was known that the Confederate army was massed at Corinth, Mississippi, just over twenty miles away.

On April 6, 1862, the Confederates attacked, surprising Grant's army and smashing it backward until the men in blue had their backs to the Tennessee River. The timely arrival of massive reinforcements and the death of the Confederate commander, Albert Sidney Johnston, allowed the US forces to regain the battlefield, but the Confederates retreated easily to Corinth.

Once more success brought jealousy; once more Grant was in conflict with his superior, Henry Halleck; and once more Grant was forced into the background while rumors of his undisciplined use of alcohol came to the fore.

Weeks of tedium and controversy passed, always difficult times for Grant, until at last he was again in the good graces of his superior officer and in command of his army. In the autumn of 1862 Grant began to move overland toward Vicksburg, Mississippi, the Confederate stronghold blocking the Mississippi River, using the railroads to build up a vast supply base at the town of Holly Springs.

In December 1862 Confederate General Earl Van Dorn made a daring raid on Holly Springs, destroying the accumulated supplies. At the same time Nathan Bedford Forrest swept across West Tennessee, wrecking the railroads leading into Memphis. Stymied in his drive on Vicksburg, Grant had no choice but to take his army back to Memphis and go into winter quarters. Again, a time of inaction gave rise to talk of Grant's drinking. At one point

Grant felt the need to write to his wife that he had been "sober as a deacon." This domestic protest raises the specter that his wife knew he was not always so sober.

The most spectacular charges about Grant being drunk concern a period in early June 1863. These charges were made by Sylvanus Cadwallader, a newspaper correspondent who claimed to have been close friends with Grant. The charges were not made in 1863 but are contained in the memoirs Cadwallader wrote, mostly without notes, in 1896. These memoirs remained in manuscript form until their publication in 1955, long after the possibility of interviewing any other eyewitnesses had faded.

Meanwhile, the siege of Vicksburg was taking place. The Union army had pinned the Confederate forces in their defenses, and nothing was happening except the dull matter of hundreds of US soldiers wielding picks and shovels, digging trenches closer and closer to the Confederate position. Almost every day reports reached the Union besiegers that General Joseph E. Johnston had raised a Confederate force that was approaching from the east to take the US troops in the rear and raise the siege. Cadwallader decided to investigate these rumors and got a small riverboat to carry him several miles up the Yazoo River to the town of Satartia, the supposed concentration point for the Southern forces.

Reaching Satartia, Cadwallader found the town empty of troops and started back downstream. Several miles later a boat was seen approaching, going upstream. When the two met, Cadwallader found Grant aboard the second riverboat. With only a single staff officer and a small escort of troops, Grant had decided to break the tedium of the siege with a personal reconnaissance to Satartia. During the conversation, as the boats bobbed side by side, Grant decided to transfer to Cadwallader's boat and continue on her, believing the vessel to be more comfortable than his own. At the time of the change of boats, Cadwallader noticed that Grant had been drinking heavily, his speech was slurred, and his stance unsteady. In a span of a couple of hours, the correspondent said, Grant made several trips to the barroom of the boat and grew increasingly drunk.

Concerned for Grant's well-being and reputation, Cadwallader convinced the boat's captain to close the barroom and then locked himself and Grant into a cabin, where he got the general partially undressed and into bed.

Also on board was Assistant Secretary of War Charles Dana, a hatchet man for his boss, Edwin Stanton. If Dana reported Grant as being on a binge, Grant's career would be over. Dana, however, chose to turn a blind eye to the situation and recorded that Grant had gotten sick and gone to bed as a result of illness.

When the boat reached Satartia, Grant woke up and had to be restrained from going ashore. Finally, with Grant back in bed, Dana ordered the boat back downstream. The next morning Grant was fully sober but did not know where he was. During the day, Grant escaped from the watchful eye of Cadwallader and again got drunk. In a desperate attempt to keep from arriving at the army's main supply base, Chickasaw Bayou, with a drunken general on his hands, Cadwallader convinced the boat's captain to run onto a sandbar. This delayed the arrival of the boat until well after darkness had fallen, but Grant was still drunk.

Once more escaping from Cadwallader, Grant mounted his horse and dashed away into the night. It took Cadwallader and

Grant's staff some time to track down the general and keep him out of sight until an enclosed ambulance could be brought to take him to the privacy of his tent.

Following this episode, Cadwallader recruited John Rawlins to send Grant a very stern letter pointing out that the general was not only risking his own reputation and career but also placing in jeopardy the fate of his army and the nation. This still didn't put an end to the rumors of drinking. The stories appeared again after Grant visited New Orleans in August 1863, and the tales were repeated again after the Chattanooga Campaign when Grant endured weeks of boredom and idleness during the winter of 1863–64.

Since the Cadwallader account did not appear until 1955, the supposed event had no effect on the course of events at the time. In 1864 Grant was made commander of all US armies and moved his headquarters to the Eastern theater of the war, where he could personally direct the fight against the major Confederate army commanded by Robert E. Lee. From May to July 1864 the contending forces faced each other daily and fought almost every day. Thousands of lives were lost, the Confederates were forced back, but still the end of the war was not in sight. By July a stalemate had developed around Petersburg, Virginia, and the two armies were locked in a siege.

June 29 was a typically hot Virginia summer day. Grant rode along the lines of his army to assess the developing stalemate. At the headquarters of three of his army corps, the commanding general took a large glass of whiskey. On the way back to his own headquarters, he had to dismount and vomit. A few days later, July 10, 1864, at the army supply base at City Point, Virginia, Grant was observed drinking with a group of other officers.

On each of these last two occasions, John Rawlins, now a brigadier general on Grant's staff, said he took charge of the situation and restored Grant to sobriety. But, despite Rawlins's best efforts, the talk about Grant being a perpetual drunk persisted, and persists to this day. What is the answer to the mystery of Grant and whiskey?

Grant had, and has, both his defenders and his critics. In biographies written as recently as the year 2000, authors have grappled with the issue of Grant's drinking. The subject is an important one and should not be ignored, nor should it be overplayed.

Alcohol was in widespread use in the nineteenth century. Grant, like many other men, was not a total abstainer; he drank liquor on some occasions. There is reason to accept as fact the idea that when lonely, bored, and depressed, Grant turned to alcohol as a crutch. No doubt, on some occasions this led to overconsumption—Grant got drunk.

Grant also suffered from severe headaches. The pain relievers available for such problems contained some potent drugs. A little ether or a small opium pill, prescribed by a medical doctor, might lead to a physical condition that an uninformed person would think indicated intoxication.

It is also a matter of historical record that much of the talk about Grant's drinking originated with people who were jealous of Grant or who thought he had done them wrong. Given the reputation he brought into the Civil War army, it was clear that rumors about Grant and whiskey would be readily accepted in many quarters. Those hostile to Grant had an easy path to follow to gain some degree of revenge.

Another major source of information about Grant and alcohol are the writings of John Rawlins and Sylvanus Cadwallader. Both of these men thought of themselves as the keeper of Grant's conscience and felt personally responsible for his successes. Of course, the more often they could present themselves as saving Grant from himself, the more important they became, not only to Grant but to the outcome of the Civil War. Their accounts are somewhat self-serving and must be evaluated with care.

However, the fact remains that Grant himself alluded more than once to the problem he had with whiskey. If we cannot accept at face value the accusations of Grant's critics, neither can we fully embrace the views of his defenders.

Did Grant drink? Yes, sometimes. Did he drink too much very often? Who knows?! Did he incapacitate himself while in command of his army? There is no clear evidence that he did. Did his drinking affect his military performance? The obvious answer is that Grant was the victor at Appomattox.

Stonewall's Lemons

N orth and South, the name "Stonewall Jackson" was legendary even as the war was being fought. Thomas Jonathan Jackson, whose campaigns are still studied in military academies around the world, became known as a brilliant strategist, but he also became known as an eccentric who, among other oddities, sucked lemons.

When the Civil War began, Jackson was an unknown member of the faculty at the Virginia Military Institute (VMI), just another ex-officer of the United States Army who had fought in the war with Mexico and then turned to other pursuits. He was not even considered an inspiring or forceful teacher; behind his back many of the VMI cadets called him "Tom Fool" or "Mad Tom." All that changed in July 1861 at the First Battle of Manassas, or Bull Run, where the soldiers of Jackson's brigade refused to retreat, "standing like a stone wall," providing a rallying point that allowed the Confederates to win a victory in the first major battle of the war. Overnight, everyone knew the name of "Stonewall"

Jackson, a hero to the South and a respected, feared opponent of the North.

From the beginning of his Civil War career, stories and rumors surrounded Jackson. It was known all over his hometown of Lexington, Virginia, that on Sundays he conducted a Bible school for African-American children, teaching them basic literacy so they could read the Bible for themselves. This was a violation of an 1832 law that forbade teaching slaves to read. It was thought that literacy might be used to plan and foment slave revolts. Jackson blithely ignored the law because he felt he owed a higher duty to God.

Shortly after the First Battle of Manassas, Jackson's pastor received a letter from the now-famous general. Thinking the missive contained news from the battlefield, the pastor called several people to come listen as he read the letter. When the envelope was opened, it was found to contain a brief note and a check on Jackson's bank. In the note Jackson apologized for having forgotten to take care of the matter earlier, but he had been busy on the preceding Sunday (it was the day of the battle) and had neglected to send his regular contribution to the church. The check for the contribution was enclosed. Not a word was written about the battle.

In the spring of 1862 Jackson's military reputation would soar higher. In command of approximately 17,000 Confederates in the Shenandoah Valley of Virginia, he would engage in a twelve-week campaign that would see him defeat three separate US commands totaling 60,000 men, a force that badly outnumbered Jackson. He marched his men 550 miles so rapidly that they became known as "foot cavalry," capturing between 4,000 and 5,000 prisoners and large amounts of stores, a success that caused a major shift in the strategy being pursued by US forces in Virginia, since President Lincoln became afraid that Jackson would capture Washington, DC.

Moving east to Richmond to join the main Confederate army under Robert E. Lee, Jackson led his men on one of the most famous maneuvers in the entire war at the end of August 1862. He took his army corps completely into the rear of the Union army commanded by General John Pope, destroying Pope's base of supplies and forcing the United States troops to fight at a disadvantage at the Second Battle of Manassas. On this occasion Jackson could have had all the lemons he wanted, since the Union supply base was stocked with luxuries private merchants had sent to their agents, or sutlers, to be sold to the soldiers.

At the Battle of Chancellorsville in Virginia, in May 1863, Jackson led half of Lee's army around the flank of the much larger Union army under Joseph Hooker and mounted a surprise attack that forced the US troops to retreat, opening the way for the Confederate invasion of the North, which culminated in the Battle of Gettysburg. At the height of his success at Chancellorsville, Jackson rode out on a reconnaissance during the night and, upon returning, was mistakenly shot by some of his own men. The wound required the amputation of his left arm. Ten days later, he died.

It is somewhat ironic that this famous military leader is associated with a most unusual symbol; in the minds of many who are interested in Civil War history, Jackson is symbolized by a lemon! A visitor to Jackson's grave in Lexington, Virginia, is likely to find several of these fruits scattered on the ground, tributes left by other pilgrims.

Is this symbol appropriate? Did the "Mighty Stonewall" really suck lemons? He was a man of many eccentricities, possessed of firm convictions, and governed by strong self-imposed rules. Jackson did suffer from poor digestion, but was sucking on lemons his favorite method of dealing with heartburn? Many believe so, but what is the basis for this belief?

The contention that Jackson loved lemons was and is accepted by many people, because he had a reputation for eccentricity. He was, indeed, a man possessed of some curious habits and he practiced these habits with a rigid self-discipline. Jackson developed his distinctive habits because he was convinced they were good for him, and this was reason enough to refuse to vary from their practice. In a letter to his sister, Laura, written in 1850, Jackson said, "It is probable that I am more particular in my rules than any person of your acquaintance."

As an example of his behavior, Jackson always sat bolt upright and would not allow his back to touch the back of his chair. His reason was the belief that his digestion only functioned properly when his alimentary canal was kept in a straight line. This adherence to a rigid posture made Jackson look rather odd on social occasions. Many people assumed his stiff posture was meant to keep companions at a distance. At a time when "paying a call" was the essence of good manners, this rule for personal health seemed to label Jackson not as one who came calling to enjoy good company, but as one who was driven solely by a sense of duty.

The diet Jackson came to favor did not make him an easy guest either. Suffering his whole life from poor digestion, the condition today known as heartburn, Jackson used trial and error to develop a diet that suited him. For breakfast he preferred a cup of black tea accompanied by a piece of wheat bread that was at least twenty-four hours old. With this he would have a small piece of broiled fresh meat (avoiding salt-cured ham or bacon) and the yolk of two eggs. He felt the whites of eggs were difficult to digest and lacking in nutritional value. Dinner, as all Southerners called the midday meal, was the same as to bread and meat but with the addition of one vegetable. The vegetable might be peas or beans or new potatoes, but the only beverage allowed was plain water. A light meal closed the day; Jackson referred to it as "tea," in something of an English fashion. This repast consisted of black tea and bread to which one could add a little butter. Fresh fruit was considered to be quite beneficial if fully ripe and if eaten before noon. Such a diet may have suited Jackson but it hardly made him a good guest at a dinner party, especially since he had regular hours at which he took his meals, and he observed these hours punctiliously.

It was also Jackson's belief that his health required him to go to bed at a set time. When he was living on a military post, bedtime was the hour at which "Tattoo" was sounded (the bugle call "Taps" was not composed until 1862). This meant that on social occasions Jackson would excuse himself and leave on the stroke of the hour, no matter what might be going on.

At some point in his life Jackson became convinced that blood accumulated in his right arm. To relieve this "imbalance" he would raise his right arm straight up from the shoulder and keep it extended until he felt he was again in balance.

Bright light hurt Jackson's eyes, but artificial light gave him a headache. In the evenings, when he wanted to review plans for the next day or when he wished to concentrate on an idea, Jackson would place a chair facing the corner of a room and sit in it to stare at the wall or at the floor for as much as an hour.

Unlike most people of his era, Jackson valued exercise and developed for himself a program of jumping, running in place, and shadow-boxing with which to keep himself in good physical condition. Today this program would be recognized as having both aerobic and flexibility benefits, but to the people of the nineteenth century, these antics merely looked weird.

Once the Civil War began, Jackson added to his personal habits an adherence to secrecy. He often frustrated his subordinate commanders by giving them the barest minimum of information about plans and intended destinations. Once Jackson said that if the coat he was wearing knew his plans, he would take off the coat and burn it. On another occasion, a fellow general asked Jackson a question about what the army planned to do. "Can you keep a secret, sir?" queried Jackson. "So can I."

Jackson was a very religious man. Even in a time and place where religion was very important and was practiced publicly, he was noted for his piety. At the Battle of Port Republic, with bullets whizzing around him and the enemy closing in, Jackson took the time to ask an officer to kindly try to refrain from using profanity while inspiring his men to fight hard. Chaplains were often invited to come to his headquarters to preach—only to see, much to their chagrin, Jackson falling asleep in the midst of their sermon.

Given these personality traits and quirks of behavior, one can understand how the "love of lemons" story caught on. It started in the postwar accounts of some of Jackson's associates.

CHAPTER 4

On May 21, 1862, Brigadier General Richard Taylor was leading his unit of Louisiana troops toward New Market, Virginia, where he had been ordered to report to General Jackson. The forces under Jackson's command were about to begin the series of marches, battles, and maneuvers that would forever after be called the Valley Campaign. Taylor, writing in 1878, described his introduction to his new commanding officer:

> A figure perched on the topmost rail of a fence overlooking the road and the field was pointed out to me as Jackson. Approaching, I saluted and declared my name and rank; then waited for a response. Before this came, I had time to see a pair of cavalry boots covering feet of gigantic size, a mangy cap, with visor drawn low, a heavy, dark beard, and wary eyes—eyes I afterward saw filled with intense but never brilliant light. A low, gentle voice inquired the distance and road marched that day.
>
> > Six-and-twenty miles, Keezletown Road.
> > You seem to have no stragglers.
> > Never allow stragglers.
> > You must teach my people, they straggle badly.
>
> A bow in reply. Just then my Creoles started their band and a waltz. After a contemplative suck at a lemon, "Thoughtless fellows for serious work" came forth. I expressed a hope that the work would not be less well done because of the gayety. A return to the lemon gave me the opportunity to retire.

Where Jackson got his lemons "No fellow could find out" but he was rarely without one.

Richard Taylor was the son of former president Zachary Taylor, so he was acquainted with many of the leading figures of the Civil War period, and he included them in his memoirs. His postwar writings are quite entertaining but contain some statements that raise eyebrows. For example, in the same passage in which Taylor presents Jackson sucking on a lemon, he claims his men's uniforms were not dirty at the end of a twenty-six-mile march made in the late-spring Virginia weather.

In the decades following the war, John Esten Cooke became one of the best-known and most widely read Southern novelists. Cooke had served as a staff officer under the command of Confederate cavalry general J. E. B. Stuart, a man both famous and picturesque. The novels Cooke wrote about the war cast a rosy aura of romance over the conflict and featured striking characters with distinctive personalities. In these novels Jackson and his ubiquitous lemon feature prominently.

Henry Kyd Douglas served on Jackson's staff from the very first of the war, and he recorded in his memoirs the following incident. It was on the battlefield of Gaines Mill, one of the Seven Days Battles fought near Richmond, Virginia, on June 27, 1862. Jackson had been conferring with General Robert E. Lee and was riding toward the battle to send his men forward:

At that moment someone handed him a lemon—a fruit of which he was specially fond. Immediately a small piece was bitten out of it and slowly and unsparingly he began to extract its flavor and its juice. From that moment until darkness ended the battle, that lemon scarcely left his lips except to be used as a baton to emphasize an order. He listened to Yankee shout or Rebel yell, to the sound of musketry advancing or receding, to all the signs of promise or apprehension, but he never for an instant lost his interest in that lemon and even spoke of its excellence. . . . When last I saw that lemon, it was torn open and exhausted and thrown away, but the day was over and the battle was won.

Douglas began writing his account sometime after the war but did not finish it until 1889. For some reason he never submitted the completed manuscript to a publisher, so that at his death in 1903 the manuscript passed into the hands of a nephew. This relative did not see fit to have the document published until 1940.

In these accounts, written long after the war and decades after Jackson's death, a legend was created. Like most legends it has some basis in fact. Jackson did enjoy lemons on occasion. While he was struggling to recover from the wound that eventually took his life, he had his wife prepare him a pitcher of lemonade, saying that she was the only person who knew how to make it to his taste; all others made the drink "too sweet." But will the use of a lemon as a symbol for Jackson withstand scrutiny? None of Jackson's close associates ever talked about him having an unusual fondness for lemons while he was alive. Asked about his love of lemons in the years after the war, Jackson's widow said she knew nothing of such a thing. What are the facts?

In 1848, as a young officer of the United States Army stationed near New York City, Jackson became quite concerned about his health. He experienced a period of rapid weight loss, dropping just over twenty pounds in a few weeks. He also found that his eyes had become quite sensitive to light. Medical doctors gave a variety of opinions regarding the cause of his condition, but there was no consensus as to what treatment should be pursued.

The nineteenth century produced a large number of quasi-scientific medical fads. Jackson, with ready access to the bookstores of New York City, began to read widely on health issues, often convincing himself that he suffered from the symptoms being described and then proceeding to try whatever cure was being advocated. In short, Jackson became a worrier over his health and showed a tendency to be a hypochondriac.

This tendency to worry over his health was especially noticeable whenever he was not kept busy and became bored.

However, it is easy to overplay the quirks of Jackson's behavior. He was happily married and treasured the time he spent with his wife and daughter. He enjoyed company, both that of adults and children. The winter before his death, Jackson made his headquarters in the office building at the Corbin plantation near Fredericksburg, Virginia. Each day when his duties were complete, he invited the five-year-old daughter who lived in the house to come to the office and spend time with him and his staff. One day Jackson took the new uniform cap an admirer had sent him and cut the lace off it to present to the little girl.

Thus, in many ways Jackson was not a man who stood out in a crowd, and his concern for his health would not sound unusual in the twenty-first century. Diet and exercise are valid concerns in any health program.

As a result of his desire for simply prepared food and healthful eating, Jackson developed and indulged his appetite for fruit—but his was an eclectic appetite. With great relish he consumed peaches, apples, grapes, pears, watermelons, and berries, all common varieties of fruit that were readily available in Virginia. And, when the opportunity arose, the general enjoyed the novelty of an orange or even a lemon.

The military exploits of Stonewall Jackson made him a legendary figure during his own lifetime. He and his men performed amazing feats of marching and fighting, so it is no wonder that legends came to cluster around him. But the facts do not support the idea that he ate lemons, or at least not on a regular basis. The stories about Jackson and lemons became popular only after he was dead and could not respond to the accounts.

Like any other lover of fruit, Jackson did use lemons, but transportation difficulties and the wartime shortages associated with life in the Confederacy made such occasions rare.

CHAPTER 5

The Legendary Courage of Alonzo Cushing

Alonzo Cushing knew he was dying. Although just twenty-two years old, he was a veteran of two years of combat and had seen men die gruesome deaths many times. He knew that July 3, 1863, was his last day on earth. The wound he had taken in his right shoulder was painful but survivable if infection did not set in; the wound to his abdomen, inflicted by a shell fragment, was fatal. He might live a few hours, perhaps even a day or two, but no surgeon with the Army of the Potomac had the skill to repair damage to the abdominal cavity.

Even so, Lon, as his friends called him, had a final, self-imposed duty to perform. Crawling painfully to the breech of his three-inch ordnance rifle, Cushing grasped the lanyard that would fire the cannon at the charging Confederate infantry. "I'll give them one last shot," he said. But before he could pull the lanyard, a rifle ball struck him in the head. Death was instantaneous.

Cushing was the commanding officer of Battery A, Fourth US Artillery. His position was in the angle formed by two stone walls near a copse of trees. The approaching Confederate infantry were making an attack that would forever be known as Pickett's Charge. Cushing fell at the climatic moment of the Battle of Gettysburg. On a field where so many acts of bravery were committed, his was among the bravest. Yet, until 2010, it had gone unrewarded.

Alonzo Hereford Cushing was born on January 19, 1841, in Delafield, Wisconsin. Ironically, he shared a birthday with Robert E. Lee, who was born on January 19, 1807. The fates of the two would intertwine at a dusty crossroads in Pennsylvania. Alonzo was the son of Milton Cushing and Mary Barker Cushing. Life for Alonzo was not easy. His father suffered from poor health and even worse business sense. As a result, the family moved away from Delafield, following a business failure, and went to Chicago.

From there Milton went to live with a relative who was a successful attorney in Vicksburg, Mississippi, hoping the climate there would improve his health. Alonzo never saw his father again. Mary moved the family to Fredonia, New York, where there were numerous Cushing relatives. There the little family was supported by the mother running a small school and the boys working at odd jobs when they were not attending school themselves. Meanwhile, Milton finally left Vicksburg but died on the trip north.

Many members of the Cushing family were successful in business and in politics. They shared an opposition to slavery but also opposed immigrants who were bringing "foreign" ways into the United States as well as spreading the Catholic faith in what was a predominantly Protestant nation. The Cushings supported the

American Party, also called the Know-Nothings since members frequently professed to "know nothing" about the party. The American Party sought to restrict immigration and to lessen the influence of new arrivals. One of the family relations, Francis Smith Edwards, was elected to Congress on the Know-Nothing ticket, and he nominated Alonzo to West Point as part of the class of 1861.

Alonzo had never particularly liked his name, and he encouraged his friends in the Corps of Cadets to call him "Lon." He worked at his studies and stood in the middle rank of his class academically, but he also played hard and earned numerous demerits for not being on time for the required formations and duties.

West Point was not immune to the tensions tearing the nation apart. As the presidential election of 1860 approached, cadets from the South and from the North tended to separate into factions that had less and less to do with each other. By the time his final year ended, Cushing saw the Confederate States formed at Montgomery, Alabama, and the first shots of the war fired at Fort Sumter in the harbor of Charleston, South Carolina. A year of academic work was compressed into a few weeks and, on June 24, 1861, Alonzo Cushing graduated from West Point and was commissioned a first lieutenant. Cushing was ordered to report to the Fourth US Artillery. He went to Washington, DC, knowing that the battery was not there—it was en route from Utah where it had been fighting Indians. For the moment the new lieutenant was assigned to Battery B, Second US Artillery.

Only a few days after Cushing reached his duty post, his unit became part of the Union advance moving toward Manassas Junction, Virginia. There, along the banks of a small stream called Bull

Run, the first major battle of the war was fought. Battery B, Second US Artillery, was not in the thick of the battle but was assigned to a place on the Union left flank at Blackburn's Ford. At that place they skirmished with Confederates commanded by General James Longstreet. Two Julys later, Cushing and Longstreet's men would meet again at Gettysburg.

The First Battle of Manassas, or Bull Run, was a disaster for the US forces. Battery B covered the retreat of the dispirited troops back to Washington, where the men took shelter inside the fortifications that had been constructed to protect the capital. Months would pass before the Union troops, under a new commander named George B. McClellan, took the field. When they did, they would move by boat to the peninsula between the York and James Rivers in Virginia. Cushing would go with them but in a new position: His new job was as a staff officer with General Edwin Sumner.

As a staff officer Cushing served throughout the Peninsula Campaign, often under fire as he carried messages across the battlefield, but without a command of his own. The campaign ended with the Union army once more in retreat. Staff duty offered little chance of promotion and less chance of deeds of daring that would draw public attention, so when Cushing was offered a field command, he took it. As the Army of the Potomac withdrew from the Peninsula to Washington, orders came for Cushing to join combined Batteries A and C, Fourth US Artillery, under the command of Lieutenant Evan Thomas. These batteries were attached to the infantry division of General Israel Richardson, a part of Sumner's II Corps.

As a subordinate officer commanding a section of two guns, Cushing marched and skirmished across Maryland as the Confederate Army of Northern Virginia moved north in September 1862. When the armies clashed along the banks of Antietam Creek near the town of Sharpsburg, Cushing's guns were in the hottest part of the action. From early morning until darkness ended the fighting, the cannon of Cushing's section supported Union attacks and helped repel Confederate thrusts. When the day was at last over, the bloodiest single day in American history had produced about 23,000 killed and wounded men. Alonzo Cushing was not among them. He came out of the fight unscathed.

The battle was a tactical draw, but Lee led his army back south, so the United States could claim a strategic victory. Lincoln seized the occasion to issue the Emancipation Proclamation, but his army commander, George McClellan, did nothing. Again the army was reorganized and a new commander was named, this time General Ambrose Burnside. In this reorganization Cushing faced a difficult decision. He was offered a position with the Topographical Engineers, another staff appointment. While such jobs held little prospect of promotion, neither did that of junior officer in an artillery battery. Cushing took the offer. Almost as soon as he had done so, he was offered his own command: Battery A, Fourth US Artillery.

Of course, Cushing wanted the battery. He sent in a request to be relieved of his engineering position, and the request was endorsed favorably all the way up the line to the commanding general of the army. Still, such things took time to traverse through the military bureaucracy, so Cushing served during the Fredericksburg

Campaign as a staff officer. The Army of the Potomac was reorganized in preparation for the upcoming campaign, with three "Grand Divisions" being created, each containing several army corps. One of the Grand Divisions was given to General Sumner, and his command of the II Corps now passed to General Darius Couch.

Because his staff was small, General Couch asked Sumner to "loan" Cushing to him. As a result, Cushing helped guide troops into position for their attack on the Confederate-held high ground. When the attack stalled in the face of the defender's fire, Cushing went into the front lines with Couch to see if anything could be done to rectify the matter. Nothing could be done. One of the Confederate defenders had noted that not even a chicken could cross their field of fire and live. The Confederate was right.

Under cover of darkness the Union army fell back to the north bank of the Rappahannock River, leaving 15,000 of their number as casualties. In the gloom of such a defeat, Cushing stayed active. As a topographical officer his duty was to scout the countryside and draw maps of what he saw. By late January, when the army attempted its next move, Cushing was tasked to lead the II Corps, since he was deemed the person who knew the country best. That this move is known to history as "the mud march" reveals its fate. The Union troops bogged down in the mud and had to get back to their camps as best they could.

When the spring of 1863 arrived, the Army of the Potomac had a new commander—again. He was General Joseph Hooker. Alonzo Cushing also had a new job, commanding officer of Battery A, Fourth US Artillery. The battery comprised some 160 men, not all of whom were gunners; many of the men drove supply wagons, served as blacksmiths, and had other non-combat roles. The weapons of the battery were six three-inch ordnance rifles. This was a very popular field piece on both sides during the Civil War because of its accuracy and reliability. With a bore diameter of three inches, the gun could fire a nine-and-a-half-pound shell over 1,800 yards using a one-pound powder charge. With a skilled gunner to aim the piece, these cannon could consistently hit a forty-eight-inch-diameter target at a range of one mile. Because the barrels of the guns were rifled, this model of cannon only fired the antipersonnel round called "canister" in an emergency. Canister was a tin can containing several lead slugs. Using such a round turned the cannon into a gigantic sawed-off shotgun, but the canister charge damaged the inside of the barrel.

As a regular army officer, Cushing was strict in maintaining discipline and often expressed his disgust at the ways of volunteer officers. When some of his men went on a drinking spree after a payday, Cushing waited until they were sober and then administered corporal punishment. Such punishment was not uncommon in Civil War armies.

On May 1 and 2, 1863, Joseph Hooker led his army into a heavily wooded area near a crossroads in Virginia known as Chancellorsville. Although heavily outnumbered, Robert E. Lee led his men to the attack. The Union army was ordered to fall back from advanced positions and to concentrate in an area near the Chancellor house. Cushing's battery was part of this move and was then taken out of the front line to become part of the reserve artillery. On May 2, when Confederates under Stonewall Jackson outflanked and routed the US right flank, Battery A remained in reserve. The next day the battery was ordered to the rear but was later returned to the front line. For three days the Army of the Potomac constricted its lines into a defensive perimeter and, on May 6, retreated north. Cushing and Battery A helped cover this move as part of the rear-guard.

At Chancellorsville the men under Cushing were not in the hottest part of the battle, and the official records show no special acts of unusual courage on any of their parts, yet a short time after the battle Cushing received a brevet (i.e., temporary) promotion to captain. It is probable that on May 2 and 3 Cushing had performed some valuable service for General Couch, who commanded the infantry unit to which Battery A was attached. The promotion seems to have been in recognition of that service. Actually, Cushing was nominated for an increase of two ranks to the grade of major, but only one step was initially approved. The second would not be approved until after his death.

Now the initiative lay with the Confederate Army of Northern Virginia. Robert E. Lee led his veterans across the Potomac River, through Maryland, and into Pennsylvania. The Union Army of the Potomac was again reorganized and received a new commanding general, George G. Meade. On July 1, 1863, the two armies converged on Gettysburg. On the way to Gettysburg, Cushing found himself under yet another corps commander, General Winfield Scott Hancock. The two men bonded quickly, and Cushing was asked to bring a two-gun section of Battery A to be part of the general's escort detail. As a result, the two men were in close company on the march across Maryland and into Pennsylvania.

On July 1 the marching men of Hancock's II Corps could hear the distant "thud" of cannon fire while still a dozen miles from Gettysburg. Then a courier on a lathered horse galloped up with a letter from General Meade. The commander of I Corps at Gettysburg had been killed in the fighting there. Hancock was ordered to turn over II Corps to a subordinate officer and to go immediately to the front to take command of all troops at Gettysburg until Meade could arrive. Hancock asked Cushing to go with him, leaving Battery A under the command of another officer. It was understood that Cushing would rejoin the guns as soon as possible.

The available records do not reveal just what Cushing did to assist Hancock that July afternoon, but General Hancock wrote out a recommendation that Cushing be promoted to the rank of lieutenant colonel in recognition of his service.

Battery A bivouacked on the field the evening of July 1, toward the southern end of the Union line. The next morning it was ordered up to the battle line to occupy a position in a pasture. In front of the battery a low stone wall ran south to north, turned east near a small stand of oak trees, then ran for some 125 yards before turning north again. The ninety-degree turn marked by the small grove of trees would be known after July 3 simply as "The Angle." Many would call it "The High-water Mark of the Confederacy." It would also be the place where the courage of Alonzo Cushing became an enduring legend.

As Battery A went into formation on July 2, Cushing placed his guns, according to regulations, some fourteen to fifteen yards apart. This meant the six cannon covered a line about seventy yards in length. The limbers, with the chest of ammunition for immediate use, stood a few yards to the rear with horses still hitched, ready to move the guns. The caissons with the reserve supply of rounds were some yards to the rear of the limbers. Wagons and non-combat personnel were sent to a safer place in the rear.

The morning was quiet for the men and guns except for brief flurries of action when they opened fire to drive back Confederate skirmishers and sharpshooters. Late afternoon changed that situation. To the left of II Corps, General Daniel Sickles, acting without orders, led his entire corps forward over half a mile to new positions. This was a dangerous move because it left both flanks of Sickles's line unsupported—"in the air" to use the Civil War term. Soon the Confederates attacked and, in an afternoon of fierce fighting, Sickles saw his corps wrecked and forced back. Battery A, and many other pieces of artillery, were called into action to stabilize the Union line and to check the Confederate advance. Several men in Cushing's command went down with wounds or were killed, and there were losses among the horses, limiting the ability of the battery to move about the field.

July 3 began with clouds, but the skies cleared as the day passed. At 8:00 a.m. a Confederate battery fired a single shot at Battery A. This shell hit a limber and exploded the ammunition in the chest. The burning fragments from the wreckage then caused two more limbers to explode. The day was not off to a good start for the men of Cushing's battery. During the rest of the morning hours, there were occasional artillery exchanges and firing off to the north near Culps Hill, but the front of II Corps was quiet. That changed suddenly.

Just before 1:00 p.m. some 150 Confederate cannon opened fire on the Union position along the central portion of Cemetery

Ridge. The first shot fired landed in the ranks of Battery A, and after that it seemed the battery and the stone wall to its front were the focus of a great deal of the Confederates' fire. Battery A suffered from this pounding. Two guns were disabled, and three others had wheels smashed.

Since the smoke was too thick to allow their cannon to be aimed to reply to the Confederate fire, Cushing would have been justified in withdrawing his men and guns behind the crest of the ridge. Some battery commanders did just that, but Cushing feared that his retreat might discourage the Union infantrymen holding the wall in front of him. This was a very reasonable assumption because the unit, the Philadelphia Brigade, had a recent history of dissatisfaction, disobedience, and low morale.

The gun crews struggled to replace the wheels under the intense fire and, while this was going on, Cushing was hit. The battery commander took two wounds in quick succession—one to the right shoulder and a mortal one to the abdomen. Then two more guns were disabled while men and horses went down.

Although his wounds entirely justified his turning over command to a subordinate and going to the rear for medical aid, Cushing stayed with his guns and his men. With only two working cannon left, ammunition low, and men decimated, Cushing made his way to General Alexander Webb, commander of the Philadelphia Brigade, whose infantrymen were posted behind the stone wall. Cushing asked the general to send enough men to man one of his guns. Webb immediately complied because he knew the firepower would aid his defense. The two remaining guns were then moved by hand forward to the corner in the stone wall now known as The Angle.

By this time the bombardment had almost ceased; only a few shots were still being fired, but long lines of Confederate infantry could be seen marching across the fields toward the battered Union position. Cushing's and other cannon opened fire, and more guns came up from the reserve to join the firing line. The volume of fire was huge, but still the gray infantry swept on. Southern soldiers were falling fast, but their momentum did not falter. At a range of about one hundred yards, Cushing gave the order to load double charges of canister, but before he could give the order to fire, he fell dead when a rifle bullet struck him in the head.

The survivors of the battery fell back, taking Cushing's body with them. Confederates overran the remaining guns, but a US counterattack soon pushed the survivors of the attack out and restored the Union lines. For all purposes the Battle of Gettysburg was over. By remaining at his post for an hour and a half after suffering a mortal wound, Cushing had helped make the victory possible.

The next day one of Cushing's brothers arrived from Washington to claim his body. On July 12, 1863, the young officer was buried with full military honors in the cemetery at the US Military Academy at West Point. His courage immediately became part of the lore of every artillery unit in the Army of the Potomac. Today, the spot where Cushing died is the single most visited place in any of the national battlefield parks.

But this legendary courage was never recognized officially. Cushing's promotion to lieutenant colonel was for work done on July 1. Why has there been no recognition of his personal courage?

That mystery, the lack of recognition, became the motivation for Margaret Zerwekh of Delafield, Wisconsin. When she found that she lived on part of the property once owned by the Cushing family, she began a crusade to have Cushing's courage rewarded. For more than thirty years, she collected material on behalf of Cushing's cause and bombarded the US Army with requests for action; she felt Cushing deserved the Medal of Honor.

The task proved difficult indeed. The first hurdle was the time. The usual process is for the nomination for the award to be made by eyewitnesses to the act of bravery; then an investigation occurs, and the award is given within two or three years. Zerwekh found that an act of Congress would be needed to waive the time limit. She enlisted the aid of Senator William Proxmire from Wisconsin to accomplish that. Even so, progress was slow.

Senator Proxmire died in 2005, and Senator Russ Feingold from Wisconsin was asked to see the project to completion. Finally, in 2010, Secretary of the Army John McHugh approved the award.

One hundred and forty-seven years after his legendary act of courage, Alonzo Cushing received recognition in the form of the Medal of Honor. The mystery is: Why did it take so long?

Author's note: Among the Confederates attacking The Angle and Cushing's guns was Private Andrew Jackson Bradley, First Tennessee Infantry, my great-great-grandfather.

CHAPTER 6

What Were They Thinking?: The Enigma of Black Slaveholders

P rivate John Wilson Buckner leaped to his feet when he heard the sentry shout, "Here they come!" followed by the long roll, the signal the drummers sounded to call the men to arms. All the gun crews belonging to the First South Carolina Artillery came pouring out of the shelters they had occupied during the bombardment laid down by US forces. Along with the rest of the 1,700-man garrison, the gunners rushed up the ramps leading to the firing platform. There they began to load their artillery pieces, ready to help repel the attack that was just beginning to take shape far down the beach.

It was July 12, 1863, and Private Buckner was one of the defenders of Battery Wagner, an earthwork fortification on Morris Island in the harbor of Charleston, South Carolina. The United States Army was beginning a months-long attempt to capture Morris Island. If successful, Union artillery could be emplaced there to bombard the city of Charleston. If the Confederates could hold the island, the civilians of Charleston would be safe.

Battery Wagner had walls 250 yards in length, reaching from the Atlantic on one side to an impassable swamp on the other. Private Buckner, and his fellow Confederates, were the cork plugging the neck of the jug from which the US troops were trying to escape.

On this day the cork held firm. Over 300 Union soldiers went down, but only a handful of Confederates did. One week later another unsuccessful attack would be launched by the United States Army against Battery Wagner. Participating in this assault would be the Fifty-Fourth Massachusetts, the first black regiment raised for service by Union authorities. The second attack is depicted in the movie *Glory*.

One of the Southerners wounded during the first attack was John Wilson Buckner. The surgeons soon assured Buckner that his wound was not fatal, though it was serious. Since he didn't live far away, he could go home to recuperate, knowing he would probably be there for several months. The thirty-two-year-old private would be glad to go home. He was a member of a wealthy plantation family who diversified their financial activities by manufacturing cotton gins. Buckner's grandfather was William Ellison, the owner of Wisdom Hall, a large, prosperous plantation near Stateburg, South Carolina, where field labor on the 900 acres was provided by seventy slaves. Buckner's uncles were also slave owners, as were he and his mother. The family estate and slave holdings placed Buckner and his family in the top 1 percent of slaveholders in the entire South.

John Wilson Buckner was black.

According to the census of 1860, there were 3.75 million people of color living in the states that would soon form the

Confederacy. Of this number, 291,988 were free. Among these "free people of color," between 2 and 3 percent owned slaves.

Slave owners were a minority across the South. In the 1860 census, 385,000 individuals were listed as slave owners. This means less than one in ten Southerners owned slaves. In the nineteenth century the head of the household was considered to own all the family's property. Some historians use a different method of assessing how many people were involved with owning slaves. These historians argue that while one person was the legal owner of a slave, all the members of the family benefited from the labor of the bond servant. Therefore, they argue, all family members should be included in the slave-owning class, even if they were not legally the owner of any slaves. Using this broader method of counting, about 20 percent of the population of the South was involved in slaveholding. This percentage includes the African-American slaveholders.

However the number of slave owners is determined, it is agreed that about 75 percent of all slave owners were small farmers. Three-quarters of all those who had slaves held one to ten slaves, with the most common number being four. Only 5 percent of those who held slaves had twenty or more bond servants. These slave owners could be called "planters" since they had a labor force large enough to farm a plantation. About 1 percent of slave owners held fifty or more people as servants. These could be called "slave magnates," and they enjoyed the lifestyle depicted in so much of the popular fiction about the antebellum South. While they dominate the popular culture about the South, they were a tiny fraction of its actual population. There are more millionaires in the South today than there were slave magnates in 1860.

The size of farms in the antebellum South reflected the size of the labor force on those farms. In 1860 the census shows that three-quarters of all farms in the South consisted of between 75 and 160 acres, the amount of land that could be worked by a family owning no slaves. Only 5 percent of all farms were 750 acres or more, and many of these large plantations included extensive acreage used as pasture, not plow land. There are more plantation-size farms in the South today than there were in 1860.

Even if one was among the minority of Southerners who owned slaves, you weren't likely to be sitting on the porch of a white-columned mansion sipping mint juleps out of a silver cup. The typical slave owner had enough labor to supplement his income but not enough labor to support him. The average slave owner needed to work in the field alongside the slaves in order to make his farm a more prosperous concern.

Only a very few lived the lifestyle so famously depicted in *Gone with the Wind.* Among those who did were some African Americans, like John Wilson Buckner and his kin, who ranked among the wealthiest people in the South—people whose wealth resulted from the labor of slaves.

Sherrod Bryant of Nashville, Tennessee, was another of the wealthy black slave owners. Bryant was born in North Carolina in 1781. When he first appears in Tennessee court records in 1806, he is described as a "free man of color," and records show he purchased land. Over the years he continued to buy plots of land in the vicinity of Nashville and, as his real estate holdings grew, Bryant purchased slaves to work on his estate.

Nashville is on the edge of the area where the weather is favorable for growing cotton, so Bryant focused on planting his land in corn. Some of this crop was consumed by his family and slaves, but much of it was used to feed hogs. Nashville not only provided a market for pork, but is also a port on the Cumberland River. Bryant was able to use the river system to ship livestock to St. Louis, Louisville, Pittsburgh, and New Orleans.

By the time of his death, just before the Civil War began, Bryant owned twenty slaves and 700 acres of land. His estate was larger than that of his famous neighbor, former president Andrew Jackson. Part of Bryant's plantation is now Long Hunter State Park. Property he once owned in Nashville is now occupied by the Schermerhorn Symphony Center.

Many of the wealthiest of the African-American slave owners lived in Louisiana. Enormous profits were made there from growing sugarcane. In 1860 there were six black slaveholders in Louisiana who held sixty-five or more slaves each. This qualified all of them to be called "slave magnates" and made each among the wealthiest people in the entire South.

Antoine Dubuclet was one of these wealthy African Americans living in Louisiana. His estate was valued at $260,000 in 1860, or the equivalent of over $10 million today.

Dubuclet was born a free man in Iberville Parish, Louisiana, in 1813. He grew up in a well-to-do family and, when of age, married into another slave-owning family. By the time of the Civil

War, Dubuclet was well established in commercial circles, with farmlands in Iberville Parish and a home and business property in New Orleans. He continued to prosper throughout the war, since New Orleans came under US occupation early in the war and trade in sugar continued to flourish. While Iberville Parish was covered by the terms of the Emancipation Proclamation, the city of New Orleans was not, so Dubuclet's estate was not affected by President Lincoln's declaration. The proclamation issued by Lincoln did not apply to areas occupied by the United States Army; it declared slaves free only in Confederate-occupied territory. It was not until the passage of the Thirteenth Amendment to the Constitution, late in 1865, that all the Dubuclet slaves gained their freedom.

Following the Civil War Dubuclet went into politics under the Republican-dominated Reconstruction government. The fact that he had been a major slave owner was not considered a problem, even in a government supported by former slaves, and he became treasurer of the state of Louisiana, a position he held from 1868 to 1878. While complaints of corruption were levied against most Reconstruction-era state governments in the South, mainly because of their spending habits, Louisiana was an exception. Under Dubuclet, the finances of the state were well managed, and he won the support of white as well as black voters. With this interracial support he continued to hold the office of treasurer even after the Reconstruction period ended.

A neighbor of Dubuclet's, P. C. Richards, and his mother, Cecile Richards, were the largest black slaveholders in the South. Their plantation absorbed the labor of 152 servants who made the Richards family a major producer of sugarcane.

To avoid the term "slave," slave owners often used the word "servant" for their workforce. In nineteenth-century usage, a servant was "one who served," and the term was applied without distinction to race or legal status. When one wished to indicate the legal status of a servant, one specified either "wage servant" or "bond servant."

Just as only a minority of white slave owners were "magnates" or even "planters," the same was certainly true of African-American slave owners. Most lived in towns and engaged in business. They owned a modest number of slaves who were engaged in assisting in the business or in performing household duties. Free men of color worked as brick masons, bakers, tailors, blacksmiths, barbers, and, along the coasts, fishermen and oystermen. In many areas free blacks had a monopoly in these crafts. All these occupations involve some unskilled labor and an assistant to perform the tasks of carrying materials and fetching supplies, which would allow the skilled workmen to work faster and earn more. Hence, the appeal of slavery to a craftsman.

This class of small slaveholders was found across the South in every town and city. In Lexington, Kentucky, a Baptist church with a black congregation found a minister it liked, but he was a slave. The congregation purchased its pastor on the installment plan. William Johnson ran a barber shop in Natchez, Mississippi, and loaned money as a sideline. His wealth accumulated to the degree that he purchased a farm and fifteen slaves. Some of this labor force worked the land, producing food for sale locally, and some assisted in the barber shop. On one occasion, Johnson sold one of his slaves to a planter in Arkansas because the servant could not stay away from Natchez saloons and was frequently drunk.

One of the leading caterers of Charleston was a free woman of color, Camilla Johnson. She purchased Diana Odd, eighteen years old, to assist her in running her catering business, which provided food for all the social events of the First Families of the city. Elizabeth Holloway made ladies dresses and was assisted by a slave named Celia. When Celia ran away to spend time with her boyfriend, Holloway advertised for her runaway slave in the local paper. When Celia was caught, Holloway had her confined in the city jail for five days and asked the police to give her twelve lashes before she was released.

There was yet another category of black slaveholder: those who purchased the freedom of a family member. There were occasions when a free person of color married a slave. On such occasions the natural action was to try to acquire enough money to purchase the enslaved partner. If the free person was in business, it was possible that the necessary money could be borrowed or saved.

After 1830, when a slave rebellion led by Nat Turner resulted in the loss of several lives, both whites and blacks, many Southern states passed laws forbidding masters to free slaves unless the newly freed slave left the state. This law meant that if one partner purchased the other, the slave partner could not be made legally free. Thus, a husband might "own" his wife. Since children took the legal status of the mother, this could also mean a father was legally the "owner" of his own children. This arrangement obviously placed a great deal of stress on the family relationship. It was, however, the best response that these people could make to the difficult circumstances presented by slavery.

In the first quarter of the twentieth century, Dr. Carter G. Woodson began to study the phenomenon of blacks holding blacks as slaves. His pioneering work focused on what he called "human-itarian motives" for the practice. Dr. Woodson's research revealed hundreds of examples of a free member of a family being the legal owner of other family members. Mosby Shepherd of Virginia told authorities of the slave rebellion being plotted by Gabriel Prosser and was rewarded with his freedom. Shepherd saved his wages and purchased his own son.

Rose Summers was a black slaveholder whose will provided for the emancipation of "my trusted servant Bella and all her children." The will also ordered the sale of four other slaves and all Summers's household possessions, with the money going to her children.

While the argument presented by Dr. Woodson is true, it is not the whole truth. Many African-American slaveholders were not motivated by humanitarian concerns. What were they thinking?

Despite its tragic implications, the matter of a spouse legally owning another occasionally produced humorous circumstances. In Columbus, Georgia, Dilsey Pope owned her husband. When her husband was found to be taking an interest in another woman, Dilsey sold him. Rough justice, but an understandable response.

As the Civil War approached, the African-American slave owners who ranked as magnates or planters found themselves facing the same issues as did their white aristocratic neighbors. If, as the abolitionists wished, the war resulted in the end of slavery, the effect on their wealth and status would be disastrous. In New Orleans and in Charleston, the black elite issued public statements siding with the Confederate cause. The Charleston statement, published in the *Courier,* said, "Our attachments are with you [the state authorities], our hope of safety and protection from you. Our allegiance is to South Carolina and in her defense we are willing to offer up our lives, and all that is dear to us."

Black plantation owners followed the patriotic course and gave up putting their land into cotton in order to plant food crops with which to fuel the Confederate war effort. At the plantation of John Wilson Buckner, the value of the food crops was over $5,000 in 1862 and again in 1863—a figure equal in today's money to about $200,000 for each year.

So, what were they thinking, these African Americans who owned black slaves? They were not innovators, because in Africa, as in Greece and Rome, history is replete with examples of people enslaving people of the same race. Nor had blacks newly come to the practice of slaveholding. Black slave owners of the Civil War period had not begun to engage in slaveholding during the "cotton revolution" that saw agricultural profits rise sharply. The practice of blacks enslaving blacks was much older. Not only did the practice exist in Africa, but during the seventeenth century a Virginia court record detailed a black man purchasing another African as a slave. At the time of the Revolutionary War, black slave owners were found in every one of the thirteen colonies.

For black slave owners there was no concern for what is today called "racial solidarity." Such a concept did not exist. There was a good deal of distrust between free and enslaved black people, with the free black community only rarely uttering concern for the plight of slaves. Being free brought obvious advantages, and wealth brought even more. Free blacks were interested in protecting these advantages and even used these advantages to exploit those at the bottom of the social structure. They, like white slave owners, were motivated by economic concerns. An exception is obvious in the case of those who owned family members, but for many African-American slaveholders the issue of economic advantage was paramount.

Twenty-first century minds may find this difficult to grasp, because slavery is now overwhelmingly thought of as a moral issue. But for most Americans in the nineteenth century, the issue of slavery was an economic question. Only a minority of citizens viewed slavery as morally wrong. This minority, the abolitionists, were unpopular in the North, because they were seen as a threat to a favorable economic situation. New England textile mills benefited from cheap Southern, slave-produced cotton. The Midwest sold much of its grain crop to Southern farmers who could plant all their land in cotton as a cash crop, purchase grain, and still make a profit.

Those who did not want slavery to spread to the new Western territories were called "free soil men." Their numbers included Abraham Lincoln. The "free soil" movement did not condemn slavery as immoral but raised economic concerns instead. A farmer employing only the labor of himself and his family could not compete with a neighbor who worked the land with slaves; a manufacturer who paid wages was at a disadvantage if his competition employed slaves. Slavery, it was argued, lowered the wages and economic opportunities for free labor.

One hundred and fifty years after the Civil War, the historical fact of African Americans owning slaves may seem like an enigma. As with so much else, the answer to the mystery can be found by following the money. For black and white slaveholders alike, the only color that mattered was green.

The Lost Confederate Gold: Following the Money

Silently the blue-clad horsemen closed in on the small encampment in the misty light of an early dawn. They could see a couple of tents, some wagons, and a few Confederate cavalrymen, some of the latter still rolled up in their blankets. A figure coming back from a nearby stream with a bucket of water saw the approaching soldiers and gave the alarm—"Yankees!"

A sudden flurry of activity erupted as men on each side reached for their weapons and raced for position; a scattering of carbine and pistol shots and then it was over. A tall, dignified man with a shawl draped around his shoulders stepped forward. "Stop shooting. It's me you want. I am Jefferson Davis."

Jubilant US troopers swarmed around the camp. This was it, the big prize. In the early dawn light of May 9, 1865, members of the First Wisconsin and the Fourth Michigan Cavalry had captured the president of the Confederate States of America. It was a month since Robert E. Lee had surrendered his Army of Northern

Virginia at Appomattox Court House and three weeks since President Lincoln had been assassinated. While some Confederate forces were still holding out in a few areas, the capture of Davis extinguished whatever flickering hope remained that some sort of long-term Confederate resistance might continue.

As the joyful Union soldiers looked over the little encampment, one thought was finally spoken aloud and passed from mouth to mouth: "Where is the money?" Ever since the evacuation of Richmond, Virginia, the Confederate capital, on April 2, rumors had been rife in Union encampments. The contents of the Confederate treasury had been loaded aboard a special train and, under guard, had been sent to Danville, Virginia. At that point, boxes, kegs, and crates full of gold and silver coins, as well as bars of bullion, had been packed into wagons and sent south. The money was to be used to bankroll Confederate resistance in the territory across the Mississippi River, it was said, or it was to finance Confederate guerrilla operations in the mountains, or—who knew what? The most interesting fact was that several million dollars in gold and silver were out there somewhere. A man who was in the right place at the right time could go home from the war a rich man.

Legally, any captured Confederate treasure would belong to the United States government as "spoils of war," but many men thought that possession was nine-tenths of the law, and if they could get their hands on Confederate gold, they had no intention of turning it loose.

The Wisconsin and Michigan troopers determined quickly that there was nothing of value in the few wagons and tents in the Confederate encampment. There was a little food and a few personal possessions, to which the soldiers helped themselves as mementoes of the occasion, but there were no wagons loaded with gold. The Confederate cavalrymen, many from Tennessee, who were guarding the presidential party, pointed out that they had been traveling light in an attempt to make a speedy getaway. They were not interested in being slowed down by heavy wagons hauling treasure.

So, where was the gold? More to the point, where *is* the gold? Coins with a face value of several million dollars in 1865 would be worth multiple millions of dollars as collector's items in the contemporary market. What has happened to the Confederate gold?

Perhaps part of the answer is to be found at the Chennault Plantation in Lincoln County, Georgia. The county is named for General Benjamin Lincoln, a hero of the American Revolution. Confederate wagon trains had passed through Washington, Georgia, in early May 1865, not many miles from the Chennault Plantation. It was near this spot that Jefferson Davis was captured.

Late on the night of May 24, Captain William H. Parker of the Confederate navy and a group of midshipmen from the Confederate Naval Academy reached the Chennault farm. Parker was a native of New York and had been a career officer in the US Navy prior to the war, but when the conflict broke out he came south and offered his services to the Confederacy while his brother remained in the US Navy. He had proven his bravery and trustworthiness over and over. At some point in the wanderings of the party he commanded, Parker had been given $86,000 in gold coins and was instructed to get aboard a ship and sail to France. There the money would be used by Confederate diplomats stranded in Europe by the end of the war. Parker had attempted to reach the ports of Augusta and Savannah but had failed in both attempts. Now he was back in the vicinity of Washington, Georgia.

Between the night of May 24 and the early hours of May 25, something happened to the gold. One account tells of it being buried near the junction of the Oconee and Apalachee Rivers, where it still lies, awaiting a lucky treasure hunter.

Another account says a group of locals, ex-Confederates and free slaves alike, assaulted the encampment, overcame the guards, and helped themselves to the gold.

It is known from official records that US troops arrested the owner of the plantation, the Reverend Mr. Dionysius Chennault, and interrogated him harshly. But, Reverend Chennault knew nothing of what had happened in the darkness hundreds of yards from his bedroom window. US General Edward A. Wild did not believe the Chennault family was innocent, especially when his men found over $110,000 in gold in the hands of local residents. General Wild went beyond harsh interrogation to actually torture the elderly clergyman. General Ulysses S. Grant, commander of all US armies, heard of the matter and ordered Wild removed from command.

Before heading to the Chennault Plantation, one should know that legend says the spot where Captain Parker and his midshipmen hid the gold is near the Parramore community in Jackson County, Florida. The Parramore community is quite near Bellview Landing, the major crossing point on the Chattahoochee River in 1865. This account says Parker was heading south in search of a quiet inlet where he might find a fishing boat that would take him to Cuba. He could then proceed with his assignment. There is only speculation as to why Parker decided to stop at Parramore, but he is alleged to have done so. At any rate, in the 1980s a couple of gold coins were found there, and the search for the lost Confederate gold has gone on in the vicinity ever since.

Unfortunately, another story places Parker and his party farther east and north, back on the Georgia side of the state line. This account relates that Parker and his party were being pursued closely by a band of renegade US soldiers, men who had gotten a taste for looting during Sherman's "March to the Sea," and who had decided to take advantage of the chaotic conditions at the end of the war to continue stealing. In an attempt to outrun this pursuit, Parker abandoned his wagon and gave each of his midshipmen a bag of gold coins. As the days went by, some of the young men, constantly on the move heading south, became exhausted and hid their bags of gold. Many tales were told in later years of elderly men, former midshipmen in the Confederate navy, wandering around the country mysteriously poking about in remote places.

According to the legend, the remainder of Parker's party camped near the junction of Mule Creek and Okapilco Creek, and during the night a band of Seminole Indians attacked the camp, killed everyone, and took the gold off to the Everglades. Of course, there is no believable account of Native Americans being in that area for over seventy-five years, and Parker lived several years after the war. But the tale of the Mule Creek Massacre is often told as the solution to the mystery of the lost Confederate gold. One also wonders how $110,000 in gold was recovered from the residents of Lincoln County, Georgia, when Parker had been given only

$86,000, especially when there is a written record of Parker return-ing his money to the Confederate treasury when he found he could not complete his mission.

Perhaps all these locations are too far south; maybe the lost Confederate treasure is in Danville, Virginia. On April 2, 1865, while attending worship services, Confederate President Jefferson Davis had received news that the Confederate battle lines near Petersburg had snapped. In a matter of hours Richmond would be in US hands. After a frantic day of packing up, Davis, cabinet offi-cers, and other officials of the Confederate government boarded a special train bound for Danville.

By the morning of Monday, April 3, space had been found in Danville for several departments of the Confederate government to resume limited operation. At the Sutherlin residence Davis con-vened a meeting of his cabinet and a proclamation was issued to newspapers declaring that the fight would go on. At this meeting, financial matters were discussed and arrangements were made to provide money for the continuing war effort. Then, it is said, thirty-nine kegs filled with Mexican silver coins were surreptitiously taken to the Danville City Cemetery and buried.

Because army hospitals were located in Danville, there were frequent burials in the cemetery. A long trench was dug, wide enough that bodies could be laid with the heads to the outside and feet overlapping in the middle. This trench was extended each day. This meant that a freshly dug section of trench would excite no comment, even if, beneath the soil, there lay treasure. The city of Danville owns the cemetery, and any request to probe the soil or to use metal detectors is met with a firm refusal. This only gives new life to speculation that the cemetery contains the lost Confederate gold.

Other accounts credit Robert Toombs as the caretaker of the treasure. Toombs was a prominent Confederate leader who lived in Washington, Georgia. He had been with Davis almost until the last day, when Toombs was given permission to return home. Years after his death the basement of his house was being cleaned out and a worker noticed that the dirt floor of the cellar sounded hollow. When a few inches of dirt were scraped away, a wooden floor was found and, beneath that, a secret room. Was this once the resting place of the now-vanished Confederate treasure?

Or, did Jefferson Davis give the gold to someone he trusted, someone who he felt would assist the South, which was in a devastated condition at the end of the war? One account has it that William S. Mumford of Waynesville, Georgia, was at a meeting of Confederate officials held at the home of Robert Toombs. There it was agreed to divide the remaining money among men who would use it for the common good. As soon as he could, following the return of peace, Mumford went to England "for business purposes." Soon after this trip Mumford began to make donations to agencies that aided orphans, widows, and disabled Confederate veterans. Descendants of William Mumford later created a college scholarship fund that continued to furnish money to needy students until 1971.

With so many stories offering conflicting details and inconclusive evidence, can we "follow the money" to find the Confederate gold? The subject is certainly fascinating. The classic Clint Eastwood movie *The Good, the Bad and the Ugly* bases its plot on a search for Confederate gold. More recently, Clive Cussler wrote an adventure novel, *Sahara,* about the missing treasure and this book also became the basis for a movie. Is there any truth to any of the stories, or is the lost Confederate gold solely the stuff of fiction?

The fact is that there are multiple "Confederate treasures." At the time of the Civil War, gold and silver coins circulated freely and were held by all banks. A large bank, such as the Bank of New Orleans, might issue its own paper money and this money would be widely accepted because the bank was known to hold enough gold to exchange paper for specie, if this was demanded. Of course, the paper bank notes were much more convenient for a person to carry. As various towns in the Confederacy came under the threat of Union occupation, the banks in those towns sent their gold reserves to a safer place. By the spring of 1862 the Bank of Tennessee, the Bank of New Orleans, and the Treasury Department of Tennessee had all deposited their gold reserves in Augusta, Georgia.

In 1860, according to the *Statistical Abstract of the US Census,* the states that formed the Confederacy included eight of the ten most prosperous states in the nation. Mississippi was the wealthiest state of all. Much of this wealth consisted of real estate, not personal property; that is, wealth consisted of land and not cash. The value of the land was tied to the crops the land produced—cotton, tobacco, sugarcane, corn—but often the cash realized from selling the crop was spent on goods manufactured in Europe or in the North. The South was wealthy, but it did not possess money. When the Civil War began, there was not a huge amount of gold in the South. This scarcity of bullion is one of the reasons the Confederate economy suffered from rampant inflation—there was little gold to support the paper currency. By the end of the war, the exchange rate was $70 in Confederate paper for $1 in gold.

As the war continued, more and more of the gold in the South came into the hands of the Confederate government as banks "loaned" their gold reserves to the national government in exchange for interest-bearing bonds. The Confederate government used the gold to purchase war materials in Europe. By 1865 there was not much gold left in the hands of the Confederate government.

In a somewhat obscure source, *The Southern Historical Society Papers,* there are two accounts that go far toward solving the mystery of the "lost Confederate gold." These papers of the society were written and published in the nineteenth and early twentieth centuries and include the accounts of eyewitnesses to Civil War events. One account concerning the Confederate gold is by John F. Wheless, a prewar banker in Nashville and the last paymaster of the Confederate navy. The second account is by Captain M. H. Clark, of Clarksville, Tennessee, who was the acting treasurer of the Confederate States at the end of the war. The two accounts are in agreement on all major details.

On April 2, 1865, two train cars were loaded with the funds remaining in the Confederate treasury. Guarded by naval personnel, this train left Richmond late at night and arrived at Danville, Virginia, early the next day, April 3. The amount of gold and silver on hand came to $327,022.90. The various banks in Richmond had placed their gold reserves on the same train to take advantage of the armed guards provided for the government funds. The gold from the banks amounted to about $300,000, but no accounting was made of this money by Confederate officials because it was private funds. The money and the party accompanying President Jefferson Davis remained in Danville for a week. Robert E. Lee surrendered his army on April 9, 1865, and the next day the gold left, moving south. It was now guarded by a small cavalry force, most of the men belonging to Tennessee regiments.

The next stop for the treasury train was at Charlotte, North Carolina, where there were organized Confederate troops commanded by General P. G. T. Beauregard. The treasury train remained in Charlotte for a week. While in this place, Secretary of the Treasury J. A. Trentholm became ill and left the presidential party. Postmaster General John A. Reagan became the acting treasurer.

As the military situation in North Carolina continued to deteriorate, officials reached a decision to move across South Carolina to Georgia. Before making this move, they paid out $39,000 to the troops in the Charlotte area. The move south passed through Abbeville, South Carolina, and halted in Washington, Georgia. There Reagan appointed Captain M. H. Clark "acting treasurer" for the Confederate government. Clark received, and gave a receipt for, $288,022.90 in remaining government funds.

While in Washington, Georgia, the officials from the Richmond banks decided to go their own way. The approximately $300,000 belonging to these banks was placed in the vault of a local bank for safekeeping. On May 4 the men in the column escorting the treasure and the remaining government officials were paid. The enlisted men received $26 each in gold and the officers more, according to the pay scale for their rank. Government officials also received their pay. Proper payroll receipts were issued in duplicate for this disbursement, which came to $108,322.90, leaving a balance in the government funds of $180,000. Another $1,800 was sent to the naval force, which had provided the original escort, and $1,454 was paid to the men guarding Davis, with $300 going to a detachment of Confederate marines.

The collapse of the Confederacy was an obvious fact, and President Davis felt a good deal of concern for the fate of the civilian population who would soon not even have the meager resources provided them by Confederate currency. It was ordered that gold and silver be sold to civilians in exchange for Confederate paper money at the rate of $70 paper for $1 gold. The defunct Confederate government had no use for the paper money, so it was burned, but at least the specie went into the hands of Southern civilians rather than being captured and taken off to Washington, DC. There are no figures for the amount dispersed in this fashion, but estimates are that it was about $75,000. This left the Confederate government with $96,946.

One of the men present in Washington, Georgia, during these tumultuous hours was Major Raphael Moses, who had been the chief commissary officer for the army corps commanded by General James Longstreet, second in command of Lee's army. Moses had proven himself to be a man capable of organizing the process by which large numbers of people were fed, and he had long since demonstrated his integrity. Major Moses was issued an order to receive $40,000 in gold and silver, which he was to accompany to Augusta, Georgia. There the money would be used to provide food and some cash for the large number of people, civilian and military, who were employed in the Confederate arsenal. Although transferring such a sum through an area where neither civil nor military law was in force was very dangerous, Moses was successful and used the money as he had been instructed.

The final disbursement made by Clark was $50,000 to "a senior naval officer." At this point the Confederacy was flat broke except for pocket change. This naval officer was likely John Taylor Wood, a native of New York who had come south at the beginning of the war because he was the nephew of Jefferson Davis. Wood was assigned the task of escorting Judah P. Benjamin, the Confederate secretary of state, to a place of safety in Europe. He was successful in this effort and never returned to the United States, living out the balance of his life in Halifax, Nova Scotia, Canada.

The money belonging to the Richmond banks was found by the US Army. The wagons carrying the gold were attacked at least twice, one of these attacks occurring near the Chennault Plantation, giving rise to the legends surrounding that location. Since the money in this cache had never been counted, it cannot be known how much was taken by the attackers, but the probable amount was close to $200,000. It is a matter of record that $110,000 was turned over to the US Treasury. Following the war the Richmond banks sued for the return of the money since it was private and not Confederate government funds. The case dragged on until 1893, when the banks got back $16,000. The court ruled the rest had been so mixed with Confederate specie at various times as to constitute "spoils of war."

Other treasure troves did crop up because banks and individuals had hidden their valuables. General Isaac Sherwood, commanding US troops near Salisbury, North Carolina, said some of his men dug up seventeen stoneware jugs holding $75,000. Almost all this money was taken by the individual soldiers who unearthed the jugs. General E. L. Molineux led US troops into Macon, Georgia. There his men seized $188,000 from the Bank of Savannah and an additional $35,000 forcibly taken from citizens. At Augusta US forces confiscated $500,000 belonging to the Bank of Tennessee. All these monies were later accounted for in proper fashion.

Can we "follow the money" to the lost Confederate treasure? In at least one case the answer is "yes." The Tennessee cavalrymen who were part of the escort of Jefferson Davis were commanded by George Dibrell of Sparta, Tennessee. These men received their last Confederate pay of $26 in the form of Mexican silver dollars. Today, in the White County Museum at Sparta, Tennessee, one of those coins is on display.

CHAPTER 8

What Became of the "Bull Pups"?

May 1865, the artillery battery of Captain John Watson Morton was camped about five miles from the village of Gainesville, Alabama. The war was over. On May 10 General Nathan Bedford Forrest, to whose command Morton's Battery belonged, had issued an address to his troops noting that an agreement had been reached with US Major General E. R. S. Canby for the surrender of Confederate troops in Alabama, Mississippi, and Louisiana. By the terms of the surrender, accurate muster rolls of each unit would be drawn up and paroles would be issued by the United States Army to each person listed. As soon as paroles were received, the men were to turn in their weapons to their own ordnance officers, and then they could go home. There would be no formal parade, no ceremony with men of both armies present; this was to be quiet and businesslike.

It took several days for the rolls to be made out, but when it was done Captain Morton took the rolls to Confederate headquarters and received the appropriate parole documents. Returning to camp, Morton assembled his eighty-plus men and gave his last order. The four guns of his battery were to "limber up" and drive to a grove of trees about a half-mile from their camp. There the guns would be parked. Any man who needed a horse was allowed to take one of those that pulled the cannon.

Following orders, the guns were deployed as directed and the men gave the weapons a last caress before riding away. Left standing in the grove were two ten-pounder Parrot rifles and two three-inch ordnance rifles. The two ordnance rifles were the most famous pieces of artillery in the Western theater of the war, known to Rebel and Yank alike as the "Bull Pups." What became of these famous guns is an unsolved mystery of the war.

Technically, the guns were called "three-inch rifles" because they had a muzzle diameter of three inches. The inside of the barrel was rifled—that is, the metal of the barrel contained grooves and lands that caused the projectile to spin in a spiral when the gun was fired. The rifling gave the piece greater accuracy. The three-inch rifle had a tube (barrel) that weighed 820 pounds, which was mounted on a wooden gun carriage. The cannon fired an oblong projectile that weighed just under ten pounds and used a one-pound charge of black powder. The range of such a projectile was 3,500 yards. These weapons were manufactured using the Rodman process, by which the gun barrels were cast around a hollow core and the mass of hot metal was cooled by circulating water through the core. This method of cooling avoided internal cracks in the barrel and produced a safer, more reliable weapon.

The two rifles left sitting in the grove had been known as the Bull Pups ever since December 1862, when Morton and his men acquired them. They had spent the war as part of the command of the colorful and famous cavalry leader Nathan Bedford Forrest. In 1861 John Morton, a then-eighteen-year-old student, had joined the Confederate army as an artilleryman. He served with distinction at Fort Donelson but became a prisoner of war when the fort surrendered in February 1862. When he was exchanged, Morton wanted to join Forrest, an officer who had led his men out of the fort rather than surrender.

When Morton reported to Forrest in November 1862, the general was not impressed. Forrest already had a good artillery commander in the person of Captain Sam Freeman; additionally, Morton was frail in build and pale of complexion. Forrest spoke of him derisively as a "whey-faced little boy" and sent him away to get an additional order from General Joseph Wheeler confirming that Morton was assigned to Forrest's command. Morton gained a degree of respect by riding one hundred miles by horseback in less than twenty-four hours to get the order.

The final act that won Forrest's approval occurred in mid-December at Clifton, Tennessee. As Forrest was ferrying his men across the Tennessee River to begin his first raid into West Tennessee, Morton approached him. "General, I have recruited twelve men, enough to man two cannon, but we have no weapons. When we cross the river me and my men intend to fight. Can you give us some shotguns?" Forrest looked intently at Morton and replied, "I'll get you some cannon." Two days later Forrest attacked and defeated the US garrison at Lexington, Tennessee. Among the spoils of war were two three-inch rifles. These were turned over to Morton and, because of their sharp, ringing bark, were soon christened the Bull Pups.

For two weeks Forrest and his men rampaged across West Tennessee, capturing Union soldiers, weapons, and materials of war. Before recrossing the Tennessee River on January 1, 1863, they had added two more cannon to Morton's command. These two guns were smooth-bores with no rifling. This meant the weapons had a shorter range, but they brought Morton's command up to full strength, allowing him to organize a battery. Barely out of his teens, Morton was now in command of four cannon, some 125 men, and a hundred horses.

Within days of organizing his battery, Morton was well on his way to becoming a favorite of Forrest's. Morton was cool under fire, brave to a fault, and obeyed orders without question. As a good officer he took care of the needs of his men and the welfare of his horses. Throughout the spring and summer of 1863, the Bull Pups were heard to "bark" on every battlefield where Forrest fought.

In September 1863 Morton took the guns into the most severe combat they had yet faced at the Battle of Chickamauga. The manner in which the battle developed required Forrest to dismount his men and to lead them into combat as infantry. The Bull Pups were placed in the battle line, and their firepower smashed back assaults, enabling the Confederate position to stand firm until reinforcements could be brought up. On one flank of Morton's Battery was the infantry of General Patrick Cleburne, perhaps the hardest-fighting foot soldiers in the Army of Tennessee. At the close of the day's fighting, the men of Cleburne's division cheered Morton's Battery. They had been concerned about having a battery from the cavalry on their flank because it was sardonically said that no one ever saw a dead man wearing spurs. But the men of Morton's command had won their admiration. Morton's Bull Pups were manned by fighters.

The day spent on the battlefield at Chickamauga was Morton's 21st birthday. At the close of the day, wearily returning to camp, he found that a mule belonging to the battery had managed to nuzzle open Morton's camp chest and eaten a new hat and jacket his father had sent him as a birthday present.

Even though now officially "of age," Morton still had a very youthful appearance. In the days following Chickamauga, General Forrest sent a courier with orders for the Bull Pups. The courier reached the guns while they were on the march, so he rode up to the nearest cannon and asked for the whereabouts of the commanding officer. The courier was directed to the man riding at the front of the column. On reaching the front of the line, the courier saw what appeared to be a boy of very tender years, not even old enough to shave. The courier rode back to the man who had given him directions and again asked for the commanding officer. This time the sergeant in charge of the cannon pointed directly to Morton. "Oh no," said the courier, "you can't pull that sort of joke on me. If I give this order to that boy Old Forrest will find out and he'll give me hell!" Appearances were deceiving. Morton and the Bull Pups understood war.

By 1864 Morton and the Bull Pups had followed Forrest to new fields of action in Mississippi. In July Forrest found himself facing superior numbers at Brice's Cross Roads. The Union cavalry was five miles in advance of the US infantry as the combat developed. Forrest decided to begin the fight early in the day, allowing him to fight and defeat the cavalry, which was equal in number to his own force. The sound of fighting would force the Union infantry to cover the intervening five miles at double-quick time. Forrest felt the fatigued condition of the foot soldiers would give him a good chance of defeating them in turn. The plan worked.

As the US cavalry was falling back, the exhausted infantry came panting up to take over the firing line. Knowing that men who had run five miles under a July Mississippi sun were probably looking for a reason to quit fighting, Forrest gave Morton the order to "hitch up your guns and, when I give the sign, charge straight down that road till you are in the Yankees' faces. Then turn loose and blast 'em." This order violated the basic military principle that artillery acting alone could not undertake offensive actions, but Morton merely saluted and told the crews of the Bull Pups to get ready. A few minutes later the order was executed and the results were what Forrest expected. The blue-clad infantry either ran or surrendered.

When asked if he was not afraid his guns would be captured and his men killed in the charge, Morton replied, "I am more scared of Forrest than I am of the Yankees."

As the Federal infantry fell back across Tishimingo Creek, which ran across the battlefield, Morton spotted two guns identical to the Bull Pups. These guns were trapped by the stampede of infantry trying to get across the narrow bridge crossing the creek. Morton asked some nearby cavalrymen to capture the pieces. Under the circumstances, this was quickly done, and as soon as the blue gun crews had been marched off as prisoners, Morton's men rushed to take charge of the still-warm guns and turn them against the retreating Yanks. This gave Morton four three-inch rifles, and he gladly turned in the smooth bores that had been half of his battery since 1862. Morton and his gunners knew these new weapons would have the range and striking power to match the Bull Pups.

In September 1864 the Bull Pups were part of an expedition Forrest was leading against the railroads along which General William Sherman shipped supplies for his campaign to take Atlanta. At bridges and other vulnerable points the railroads were protected by blockhouses. These structures were built of timbers eighteen to twenty-four inches on each side, with earth piled against the outside to a height of four to five feet. Loopholes were left for the garrison to fire through to protect themselves and the railroad structure. These blockhouses were excellent defenses against guerrillas or cavalry patrols that penetrated Union lines.

Forrest, at the head of a regiment of cavalry, came in sight of such a blockhouse near Athens, Alabama. Stopping just out of rifle range, he sent forward a flag of truce carried by an officer who demanded that the US soldiers in the blockhouse surrender. The commanding officer, thinking he was dealing with just another cavalry patrol on a scouting expedition, haughtily refused the demand. Morton then brought up the Bull Pups and, at a range of 800 yards, knocked a timber out of the blockhouse wall at the first shot. A white towel was immediately waved from a loophole. Forrest turned to Morton and laughed. "Fire another shot just over their heads, John. After the language that fellow used, it will take a bed sheet to get my attention." A second shot produced a much larger flag, and the surrender was accepted.

When the next blockhouse was reached, a few miles farther along the track, the officer who had surrendered the first position was sent forward with the Confederate bearing the flag of truce. All other blockhouses surrendered without a fight. Even massive wooden timbers and earthworks were no match for the Bull Pups.

These were the famous artillery pieces left glinting in the sunlight in a grove of trees near Gainesville, Alabama, in May 1865. No US soldiers were present at the surrender of the guns. The Federal authorities were showing their respect for the defeated Confederates by allowing them to leave in private. These were the only cannon whose nicknames were known to both armies—they were the most famous pieces of artillery in the Western Confederacy. After their gunners rode away, what happened to them?

After the surrender of Confederate forces, the weapons that had been given up were collected and sent to various US arsenals and warehouses. Some of the material was sold to other nations, but muzzle-loading rifles were obsolescent by 1865. Metal cartridges and repeating rifles were already coming into use, and these improved weapons soon replaced the Springfield and Enfield rifles that had been so widely used during the war. Muzzle-loading artillery held on a little longer, but it was not in use in the field by the time of the war with Spain in 1898. The old Civil War artillery began to be sold in the latter part of the nineteenth century to towns that wanted a cannon or two to put in position as part of a war memorial. Chickamauga became the first national battlefield park, established in 1890, and more cannon were sent there to mark troop positions. Other parks absorbed more of the old guns when they were established.

On the field of Chickamauga, at the location where Morton's Battery helped hold the line, are two three-inch rifles. It is entirely appropriate that this caliber of gun should mark this location, but visitors often ask, "Are these the real Bull Pups?" After all, John Morton came to the proposed park and, in company with veterans of both sides, walked over the field helping park officials locate significant sites. Perhaps Morton had kept track of the Bull Pups all these years and used his friendship with the park superintendent, Alexander Peter Stewart, a former Confederate general, to have the guns put back where they had once been used in battle. Park rangers say no, that the serial numbers on the cannon are not the same as the guns once commanded by John Morton. But, the story persists that these are the Bull Pups. After all, no one has ever produced the written record showing the serial numbers of the guns captured at Lexington, Tennessee, in December 1862.

John Morton returned to the family home in Nashville when the war ended. Morton's father was a leading physician in Nashville, and the son decided to follow in his father's footsteps. One result of the war was that there would be a demand for years for doctors to treat the lasting effects of wounds. Continuing his interrupted education, Morton enrolled at the University of Nashville in the fall of 1865. The medical school of this institution had a well-trained faculty and a good reputation stretching back to the antebellum period. The course of study was thirty months, and Morton's class graduated at the end of February 1868. There were fifty-six graduates in the class, and Morton was the valedictorian. He then took up the practice of medicine with his father. There were a great many patients but not much money, so Morton planted grapes on part of the family farm and began the production of wine.

John Morton was prominent in his opposition to the Republican Reconstruction government and was influential in politics once the Democrats returned to power in 1869. According to Morton's own testimony, he was a member of the Ku Klux Klan. The family farm was an easy ride by horse or streetcar from downtown Nashville, and it was a gathering place for veterans of Forrest's command. It was at "Vine Hill" that plans were made to organize the Tennessee Division of the United Confederate Veterans. The surviving members of Forrest's staff and escort (bodyguard) company held one of their reunions on the farm.

Old Confederates who visited Morton's home recall that for many years two three-inch rifles sat on the lawn of the house. When asked if these were the Bull Pups, Morton would always laugh and change the subject. Morton was something of a minor historian of the war, especially of events in which his battery and the Bull Pups were involved. He wrote articles for *Confederate Veteran* magazine and submitted papers to the Southern Historical Society. While Morton was proud of his war record and of the exploits of the Bull Pups, he never hinted at the ultimate fate of the guns—if, indeed, he knew what that fate was.

In 1901 Morton became secretary of state for the state of Tennessee. A few weeks before he was to leave office in 1909, the guns disappeared from the lawn of his home. That weekend a crew of masons worked in the basement of the State Capitol, walling off an alcove in the sub-basement. There is no public access to that part of the building. The question arose soon after Morton left office: "Is this the last resting place of the Bull Pups?" More than a century after Morton left office, the chief architect for the Capitol says there is no record of any wall being built in the sub-basement in 1909. But, no one is allowed to go into the area to see if any wall sounds hollow when struck with a hammer.

What happened to the Bull Pups, the most famous cannon in the Western theater of the Civil War? Do they stand on the field at Chickamauga? Are they secreted away in the bowels of the Tennessee Capitol? Were they melted down for scrap? No one knows. But on a still day in a quiet corner of any field where men once fought, an ear attuned to history can still hear the Bull Pups bark.

Battlefield Hospitals and Civil War Medicine

The rifle slug hit the soldier's leg with the force of a mule kicking him. His hat flew off, his rifle slid from his hands, and he crumpled to the ground. Blood gushed through the torn fabric of his uniform pants but, as yet, there was no pain—just the numbness of shock.

Four of his friends left their places in the firing line. One of them took the blanket the fallen soldier used as his bedroll, and his friends, spreading the blanket on the ground, moved the prostrate man onto it. A gasp escaped his lips as they did so and another followed as each man lifted a corner of the blanket and set off for the field hospital whose location was marked by either a solid red or a solid yellow flag.

At the field hospital, which might have been nothing more than a swale in a pasture, somewhat out of the line of fire, the man on the blanket was placed on the ground, and his friends soon left to return to the firing line, or, if they were not very good soldiers, to find a secluded spot from which to watch the rest of the battle.

Now the shock was wearing off and the pain was beginning. Unable to help himself, the soldier shook with sobs and gasped in his suffering. Out of the corner of his eye, he could see the surgeons at work on other patients. All they seemed to do was cut and saw, cut and saw, while a pile of severed limbs grew steadily on the ground near them.

The sounds coming from the vicinity of the surgeons could not be described, and the wounded man did not want his turn to come. Soon enough, though, it did. Rough hands picked him up from his blanket and slapped him down on a blood-slick table. "Put a leather strap in his mouth so he won't bite his tongue and hold him still," said the surgeon.

Mercifully, it took less than a minute. His leg was gone to join the pile of limbs on the ground. The soldier was taken to one side to become part of a lengthening line of men lying in the sun. Flies buzzed and swarmed over the fresh incision. Thirst grew and became unbearable. Hunger began to gnaw. The stink of unwashed bodies, of blood and feces and urine grew. But no one came, only the patient buzzards circling slowly in the sky, waiting, waiting . . .

Such is the popular image of a Civil War army hospital, a legend reinforced by dozens of B-grade movies and hundreds of paperback novels. A lot of blood and gore, perhaps a little whiskey to take the edge off the pain, and a bloody-handed butcher who had little or no training in medicine but who was gaining a lot of experience in amputation. This is the legend of the Civil War hospital.

Legends do tend to have some basis in fact, but they also depart from reality rather quickly. Our picture of a Civil War hospital is no exception. Actual photographs of these facilities are available; well known and talented writers such as Walt Whitman, Clara Barton, Kate Cumming, and Louisa May Alcott all wrote vivid descriptions of their experiences working in Civil War hospitals. For the most part, these people were located far behind the battle lines but occasionally they were within the sound of the guns. Walt Whitman knew just how bad conditions in hospitals could become, yet he said of the doctors who staffed them, "All but a few were excellent men."

At the time of the Civil War, medical science was poised on the verge of a great leap forward, but it had not yet made that leap. Nearly all the older doctors had learned their craft as apprentices. Medical schools were still a rather recent innovation and, when an aspiring physician did attend one, the term of study was only two years, sometimes one. Harvard University did not have a single stethoscope or microscope in its medical department prior to the war. Some advanced thinkers in the field of medicine were beginning to discuss the germ theory as the basis for spreading disease, but bad air or bad water were still more likely to be considered the cause of illness. There was no concept at all of sepsis, so sickrooms, doctor's offices, and sites for operations were dirty as a matter of routine.

Although the United States Army had fought a war with Mexico from 1846 to 1848 and although troops were on active duty against various tribes of Native Americans, little attention was paid to medical affairs in the military. In 1860 the entire professional medical staff of the US Army totaled 114 men. There was a surgeon general, thirty surgeons who held rank equivalent to major of cavalry, and eighty-three assistant surgeons who held rank equivalent to captain of cavalry. The cavalry equivalency allowed the doctors to have a horse, draw forage for the animal, and have a baggage wagon and team assigned them for medical supplies.

When the Civil War began, the members of the Medical Corps split in their allegiance, just as the officers of the line did. Twenty-four of the surgeons and assistant surgeons resigned from the United States Army to support their native states. One of these was Dr. Samuel Preston Moore, who served as Confederate surgeon general from July 1, 1861, until the end of the war. Having spent twenty-seven years in the US Medical Corps, Dr. Moore had very definite ideas as to how to organize the Confederate medical department. Fortunately, many of his ideas were quite good and represented advanced medical thinking for his day. Moore set up Boards of Examination to test the knowledge of would-be Confederate doctors; he railed constantly on the topic of keeping troop encampments clean; and he insisted that when buildings were constructed for use as hospitals, they be well ventilated.

Just as President Lincoln found it difficult to find an effective commanding general for his fighting forces, so he experienced difficulty in finding competent medical leadership. The US Medical Corps was dominated by men in their seventies and eighties who had not had a new medical idea in decades, who wanted to maintain the status quo of medical practice, even when it obviously did not work, and who were more concerned about saving money than they were about saving lives.

Eventually, Dr. William A. Hammond was chosen to serve as surgeon general. Hammond was an efficient man who attempted to standardize practices in order to meet the challenges of a major war. He wrote new textbooks on military medicine and produced a field manual to be used by hospital stewards on active duty. However, Hammond drew the ire of the "old guard," who wanted nothing changed, and he lasted just over a year in his office.

The best work on the Union side was done not by the Medical Corps, but by civilian volunteers, especially the Sanitary Commission. Loosely based on a British volunteer service that had assisted during the Crimean War, the US version was headed by Henry W. Bellows, a prominent Unitarian minister, and Henry Law Olmstead, the landscape architect. Ironically, the Sanitary Commission was to limit its aid to volunteer regiments from each state and to have nothing to do with the regular army.

The Sanitary Commission set to work creating local branches throughout the North, collecting food to supplement the rather coarse rations the army provided to the hospitals. The commission provided volunteers for rear-area hospitals and even provided hospital ships to be used to evacuate the wounded from coastal and riverine areas.

The South never created an agency as large and efficient as the Sanitary Commission, but in areas near large permanent hospitals, similar efforts were made. While it was rare to find a civilian in a battlefield hospital, the rear-area medical facilities, North and South, benefited from private efforts.

For Johnny Reb or Billy Yank, what did medical care mean on a day-to-day basis? Every morning, shortly after reveille, the drum or bugle would sound "Sick Call." The men who assembled in response to the signal were marched by the first sergeant to the regimental hospital. This was usually nothing more than a wall tent that could hold eight or ten men. At the regimental hospital the assistant surgeon examined the men and passed judgment on their condition. Some were put on a cot in the hospital tent where they could receive medicine, but others were given a dose of drugs and sent back to their own quarters. Others might receive light duty to allow more time for rest, while some were discharged and sent back to regular duty.

Most of the problems seen by the assistant surgeon at morning sick call were digestive or respiratory in nature. Most of the digestive problems were caused by contaminated water and poor diet. The armies of the Civil War crowded large numbers of men and animals into relatively small spaces. With rather vague ideas about the deleterious effects of contamination, the armies found no effective way to prevent human and animal feces from contaminating groundwater or even wells. Since most drinking and cooking water came from creeks and streams, it was frequently the case that morning coffee was more like fecal soup. As a result, men by the thousands suffered from chronic diarrhea. Chimborazo Hospital in Richmond was the single largest Confederate hospital, and during the course of the war over 70,000 patients came through its doors. Over 10,000 of them had chronic diarrhea. Experts estimate that 95 percent of all Civil War soldiers had this problem, to a greater or lesser extent, at some time during the war.

Poor diet contributed to digestive problems. Rations were long on calories, short on vitamins. Beef, fresh or pickled; salt-cured pork; dried beans; coffee; and hardtack constituted the typical daily ration. Hardtack was a cracker about four inches on each side and one-half inch thick. It was made primarily of flour, sugar, and shortening. Twelve of these crackers were the standard issue for one day. These crackers were high in carbohydrates and provided quick energy, but they left a lot to be desired in nutritional values.

Because the hardtack was often weeks or months, if not years, old, it was sometimes impossible to chew. Soldiers resorted to soaking their crackers in water while frying their salt pork. The soggy crackers were then fried in the pork grease and washed down with strong black coffee. The great wonder is that all armies did not collapse with indigestion!

With less than clean water and a diet of fried food, it is no wonder the assistant surgeon of each regiment saw so many cases of digestive disorders. One doctor later recalled that he carried only two medicines to morning sick call—blue mass to cure constipation and opium to treat diarrhea.

There were also routine injuries. The infantrymen got blisters and twisted ankles. Artillerymen sometimes got smashed toes by failing to get out of the way of a gun when it recoiled after being fired. One surgeon reported he treated only one wound inflicted by a sword during the entire war, and it was the result of an accident that occurred during a drill. In all, more than twice as many men died of ordinary sickness as lost their lives in battle.

Battlefield medicine was far more spectacular and more fearsome than the day-to-day routine of medical care. Small-scale actions might suddenly flare up, but in the Civil War larger battles usually were preceded by days of maneuver during which the armies drew closer together. Most often, there was time for some preparation by the medical corps.

When the infantry marched into battle formation and the artillery rolled into position, the assistant surgeon of each regiment and one man chosen for the purpose of accompanying him would go behind the battle line to establish an "advance," or dressing, station. This was often just behind the firing line by a hundred or so yards, perhaps in a building or in a protective fold in the terrain. The location would be marked by a "hospital flag," which was solid red or solid yellow. The members of the regimental band would put away their instruments and take up stretchers, for their job now was to transport the wounded from where they fell to the doctors. Combat officers discouraged the practice of comrades taking a wounded friend to the rear; they said that this was too convenient a chance to leave the firing line and that poorly motivated men never came back until the battle was over.

At the advance station, the assistant surgeon and his steward would have whiskey or brandy available in a knapsack, opium pills, and bandages. When a wounded man walked back to their position, or was carried in by stretcher bearers, the assistant surgeon and steward did all they could to alleviate the pain and to stop the bleeding. Often the only treatment for a wound was washing it by pouring water over it, wrapping it tightly in bandages, and giving the wounded man a drink of liquor as a stimulant. Painkillers could be given if it was thought advisable. Ambulances or wagons might come forward to assist in evacuating the wounded, but only when the course of the battle would allow movement so far forward.

Very early in the war it became customary to group all the regimental hospitals for a single brigade together. This spread the workload among more doctors and even allowed a degree of specialization. Although tents were provided for the use of brigade hospitals, it was often the case that houses, barns, churches, and schools were used for this purpose. Most brigade hospitals were located about one-half mile to one mile from the advance station. Again, the location was marked with a hospital flag. Walking wounded, stretcher bearers, and ambulances or wagons converged on this location with their loads of wounded.

At the brigade hospital triage was performed, since first aid had already been given at the advance station. A doctor examined each case. If soldiers were determined to have only flesh wounds, they were given some opium pills for the pain and placed to one side for attention later. They were in no immediate danger and could wait for assistance. Those men with abdominal wounds and head wounds were made as comfortable as possible and were then left to the care of hospital stewards who were assisted by the walking wounded. The wounds these men bore were at the outer limits of medical science's ability to provide treatment. It was almost certain these men would die within a few days, no matter how much time the doctors spent with them. Once all the other wounded had been treated, the doctors would return to these cases, and if any of the patients were still alive, would do what they could, which was usually not much. In the meantime, opium pills or laudanum (opium dissolved in alcohol) would be administered.

The men who would receive immediate treatment were those who had been shot in the extremities—arms or legs. If these wounds could be dealt with before gangrene set in, there was a good chance the patient would survive. A very likely treatment for such a wound was amputation.

Civil War rifles fired large—.57- or .59-caliber—and relatively slow-moving soft-lead bullets. When one of these slugs struck a human body, it tended to mushroom, making a wound that grew larger as it went deeper. Because it was slow moving, the projectile tended to stay inside the body rather than make an exit by passing all the way through. Of course, the mushrooming bullet carried into the wound shreds of the clothing through which it passed, creating a prime source for infection. If the slug struck a bone, instead of a clean break, there would be shattering or splintering for some distance above and below the point of impact. With no way to remove or to replace the splintered bone, the doctor faced the certainty of a fatal infection. Removing the injured limb before it became infected could give the patient a chance of survival.

The frequently repeated descriptions of brigade hospitals featuring a pile of severed limbs are very much an accurate account of a Civil War hospital scene. The picture is, however, not one of butchery but of the best medical practices of that time. The United States Army Medical Corps records for the Civil War are relatively intact. They show 175,000 wounds to extremities among Union troops. Of these, 30,000 led to amputation. About 70 percent of those who had an amputation survived. The records for the Confederate army are not nearly so complete, but the same general percentage of amputations and survival seems to hold true.

The Battle of Franklin, November 30, 1864, was one of the bloodiest fights of the entire war. At daylight on December 1, Dr.

Deering M. Roberts established a hospital for the wounded of the division commanded by Confederate General William B. Bate. Dr. Roberts commandeered an old carriage and wagon shop, a store, and the chancery courtroom. Hospital stewards removed all furniture and trash, cleaned the areas, and spread clean straw over the floors to a depth of twelve inches. That same day wounded men began to arrive from the actual battlefield. Over the next twenty-four days, only seven men died in this hospital. Two died of abdominal wounds, three of head wounds, one of an amputation, and one of infection when he refused an amputation. On December 25 all the patients were well enough to be moved, and they were taken to Nashville since they had been captured when the Confederate army retreated.

As soon as possible our wounded Johnny Reb or Billy Yank would be sent further behind the lines to a "general hospital." There they did not limit admissions on the basis of medical problems, so a wounded man might find himself a neighbor to one who was ill. Following a major battle, however, the general hospitals tried to clear room for the wounded by asking local families to take in recuperating men.

In cities such as Richmond, Washington, DC, Indianapolis, and St. Louis, general hospitals were established in buildings constructed for that purpose. These structures were long, open rooms called "pavilions" with lots of windows to provide air circulation, while vents in the roofs allowed some of the summer heat to escape. Toilets were provided in each pavilion, although supplying water to keep these flushed and scrubbed was a problem. The pavilions radiated from a central building like spokes of a wheel from a hub. The central building was the kitchen, medical offices, and storehouse for drugs.

Since many of these permanent structures were in large cities, it was here that civilians, including women, could be found assisting the wounded. Some of those who volunteered were well known. Dorothea Dix had earned a prewar reputation as a reformer of jails and as a founder of mental hospitals. Her personality made her a difficult partner, and army surgeons expressed strong dislike for her and for her nurses.

By September 1863 many single young women were working in general hospitals. Most of these did little nursing, in the medical sense, but they provided cheerful companionship that was of vast psychological benefit to the wounded soldiers. Among many small kindnesses, they read to the wounded, wrote letters home for them, and brought flowers into the wards.

The most colorful of the women hospital workers was Mary Ann Bickerdike, a widow, who visited a Union army camp at Cairo, Illinois, in 1861, "just to see how she could help." By the end of her career she had nursed the wounded on nineteen battlefields and had helped set up more than 300 hospitals.

Phoebe Yates Pember was a young widow who dedicated her life to caring for the wounded who were sent to Richmond's Chimborazo Hospital. From 1862 until the end of the war, she nursed and supervised the nursing of thousands of wounded men.

Kate Cumming was born in Scotland but was living in Alabama when the war began. By the spring of 1862 she was in Corinth, Mississippi, caring for the wounded from the Battle of Shiloh and the even more numerous sick Confederates. Throughout the war

Cumming traveled to the nearest Confederate general hospital she could find to do what she could.

These are only a few of the examples of the hundreds of women, North and South, who responded to the public call and to their private urge to "do something" to help.

Neither Johnny Reb nor Billy Yank would have looked forward to a trip to a hospital, but who does even now? But when it became necessary for Civil War soldiers to seek medical services, they found waiting for them not butchers but men and women ready to do the very best they could. If the medical methods of the era seem crude and the treatment harsh, we must remember that we cannot judge the people of the past by the knowledge and standards of today. Those Civil War doctors took the same oath a physician takes today: "First, do no harm." As best they could, they provided for those under their care.

CHAPTER 10

The Mysterious Sinking of the Hunley

Late on the night of February 17, 1864, a blue light could be seen out beyond the entrance to Charleston Harbor. Earlier a flash of fire had been glimpsed, and some said they had heard a muffled explosion. The blue signal light was significant. It was the prearranged signal that *H. L. Hunley* had been successful in its mission. The blue light meant a warship had been sunk by a submarine craft. *Hunley* had just sent the USS *Housatonic* to the bottom of the Atlantic. Then the waiting began. The Confederate authorities waited and waited, but *Hunley* did not return. History had been made, but a mystery had been created.

In the midday sun of August 8, 2000, the cigar-shaped hull gradually emerged from the gloom of the ocean depths. Suspended from nylon slings and cradled in a truss of steel pipes, padded with rubber bags filled with foam, *H. L. Hunley* was lifted aboard a salvage barge and began to move toward shore. Appropriately, the salvage barge displayed prominently a blue light. *Hunley* was coming home.

Among the many mysteries awaiting solution was the key issue of why the *Hunley* sunk.

The beginning of the Civil War presented the Confederacy with an immediate and pressing problem. Only 20 percent of the manufacturing capacity of the United States was located in the states that left the Union. This meant the fledgling nation would only have limited means with which to produce the materials for conducting a war.

The South did have plenty of the valuable commodity of cotton, much in demand in British textile manufacturing centers. Cotton could be sent to Europe, sold there, and war materials purchased for shipment to Confederate ports. The US response to this was to declare a blockade of the Confederate coastline to shut off this potentially potent flow of trade and supplies. The blockade would not win the war by a single, spectacular victory, but it would slowly strangle the economy of the South and, with it, the ability of the Confederacy to make war.

An often-used phrase speaks of "Yankee ingenuity." It would not be amiss to talk about "Rebel ingenuity" when one considers the Confederate response to the blockade. Underwater mines, then called "torpedoes," were developed and deployed to protect harbors; ironclad ships, such as the CSS *Virginia,* were built; and submarines were designed, constructed, and sent to sea.

One of the "ingenious Rebels" was Horace Lawson Hunley, a native of Sumner County, Tennessee, who had moved to New Orleans. In that city he developed an interest in marine engineering, although he practiced law to earn his living. Hunley had served in the Louisiana legislature, so he had the political contacts to assist him in working with the Confederate military. Sometime in the summer of 1861, Hunley met James McClintock, owner of a machine shop. The two men saw an opportunity to aid the cause of Southern independence and make some money while doing so.

The Confederate government, lacking a navy, had turned to an old idea, that of privateers, to find naval resources. The Confederate government would issue a license, called a "letter of marque," to private citizens, authorizing them to attack ships flying the flag of the United States. If privateers captured a ship, they could sell the vessel and its cargo. Of course, the Confederate government would immediately purchase any war materials. If a US warship was sunk, the privateer would receive a hefty cash reward. Hunley and McClintock decided to go into the business of building an unusual privateer.

Hunley had ideas and contacts, both political and financial; McClintock had manufacturing experience and building capacity. This partnership produced a small, submersible craft, the *Pioneer*.

This early version of a submarine was constructed from an old boiler taken from a steamboat. The *Pioneer* was about thirty-four feet in length, just over four feet in width, and four feet in height. Two crew members sat in the body of the craft, turning a crank that spun the propeller. A captain stood in a small conning tower and steered the craft by pulling on ropes attached to the rudder. Diving fins attached to the side could be tilted to make the boat go under the water or to cause it to move toward the surface.

Pioneer made several test runs and proved her ability to dive and to surface, but neither the ship nor the crew was ready for combat when the United States Navy ran the gauntlet of the forts guarding the Mississippi River and steamed upriver with a convoy of soldiers to capture New Orleans. *Pioneer* was sunk by her builders, and the construction team moved to Mobile, Alabama.

In Mobile, the New Orleans team contacted a machine shop owned by Thomas Park and Thomas Lyon. These men were agreeable to becoming involved in the project, as were two members of the Confederate army who were on leave following the Battle of Shiloh. William Alexander and George E. Dixon, both members of the Twenty-First Alabama Infantry, had been given medical leave to recover from wounds. Alexander was an immigrant from Britain who had been in the States for several years, while Dixon was a native of Kentucky.

The design Hunley submitted to Park and Lyon for construction kept several of the features of *Pioneer*. The diving fins were seen to be a workable solution to making the craft go up and down, and the screw propeller worked well. The size of the crew was increased to four and the crankshaft redesigned accordingly. A more streamlined shape was created to facilitate passage through the water. The craft was named the *American Diver*. On February 14, 1863, the crew went out on its first combat mission and disaster immediately struck. Rough seas broke over the craft before the watertight hatches were secured, water accumulated faster than it could be pumped out, and *American Diver* sank with all hands in Mobile Bay.

Hunley and McClintock were dismayed but not defeated. By the summer of 1863 they had designed, and Parks and Lyon had built, a third submarine. This one had no name yet, but it incorporated all the technological discoveries from its predecessors. Hunley needed money for this effort, and the Confederate government purchased shares in the venture. The government agency involved was headed by E. C. Singer and was engaged in the development of several secret weapons for the Confederates.

Then destiny called. In Charleston, South Carolina, General Pierre G. T. Beauregard, the Confederate hero of the capture of Fort Sumter and the victor at the Battle of First Manassas, heard about the new boat that could swim and dive like a fish. Charleston, on the Atlantic, was of more strategic importance to the Confederacy than was Mobile on the Gulf of Mexico. Since the government owned the majority of the shares in the boat, Beauregard ordered her brought to Charleston. Hoisted out of the water, the "fish boat" was loaded aboard flatbed railcars, and the train chugged off to Charleston, accompanied by Dixon and Alexander.

Conditions in Charleston were stressful. The United States Army and Navy bombarded the city at random intervals, making life anywhere along the waterfront of the city dangerous. Technical difficulties beset the fish boat, and personality conflicts flared up. In the midst of these conditions, the Confederate army seized control of the boat and fatal accidents began to occur.

On August 29, 1863, Lieutenant John Payne of the Confederate navy was in command of the boat. In the process of casting off a towline attached to a steamer that was pulling the boat into deep water, Payne accidentally stepped on the lever that controlled the diving fins. The hatches were open as the boat went under and water poured into the hull. The boat did not have a great deal of buoyancy, and it took little water to send it plummeting to the bottom of the harbor. Four members of the crew managed to scramble out of the hatches against the stream of water entering the boat, but five men drowned.

Horace Hunley was distraught. He felt the government had taken over his boat and had caused an inexperienced crew to be placed aboard with fatal consequences. Hunley asked that control of the boat be returned to him and that he be allowed to choose a crew, preferably men who had served with him in Mobile. This was done. On October 15, 1863, Hunley and his picked crew took the boat out on a training exercise. As part of the exercise, a dive was made under a ship that served as a mock target. The fish boat approached and dove, but it did not come back to the surface on the far side of the ship.

Nothing could be done to effect a rescue, and it was three weeks before a team of divers located the boat, attached cables, and hoisted it to the surface. The fish boat had dived so steeply and so strongly that she had buried her nose in the mud of the harbor bottom and could not force herself loose. The bodies of the crew were buried with military honors, even though Hunley was a civilian.

General Beauregard had seen enough. Although the vessel was formally christened the *H. L. Hunley*, it was ordered docked and was hoisted out of the water. George Dixon had other ideas. Working with his old friend, William Alexander, and a crew of volunteers, *Hunley* was cleaned up and refurbished. Practice runs resumed and, by February 1864 *Hunley* and her crew were ready. Of course, all this had not gone unnoticed, and reports about *Hunley* had reached the United States Navy blockaders. Orders had been issued by the admiral in command to see that each ship took additional precautions against attack. These included anchoring each night in shallow water to make it more difficult for a submersible craft to dive beneath them so as to plant an explosive device under their hull.

On the evening of February 17, 1864, Lieutenant George Dixon took *Hunley* out to do battle. Just past 8:30 p.m. *Hunley* approached the USS *Housatonic*. Lookouts aboard the ship spotted the approaching submarine on the surface but at first passed it off as a log. Fifteen minutes later, the "log" had slipped to the side of *Housatonic,* bumped the ship, and began to back away. Moments later an explosion ripped through the hull of the warship. Some of the crew fired small arms at *Hunley,* but she was so close to *Housatonic* that the ship's big guns could not be depressed sufficiently to hit the attacker. With a large hole blown in her hull, *Housatonic* rapidly sank to the ocean floor twenty-five feet below. Only five sailors died, the rest scrambling into the rigging that rose well above the water. Boats were launched from nearby blockaders, and the crew was rapidly rescued.

On shore, the Confederates could see the ships of the blockading fleet signaling each other and milling about. Some saw the blue light aboard *Hunley.* Then the light winked out. Mystery would envelop *Hunley* for the next 131 years.

Clive Cussler had dealt with underwater activity, both imaginary and actual. A best-selling author of adventure novels with lots of underwater activity, Cussler is also the founder of the not-for-profit National Underwater Marine Agency (NUMA). Working with marine experts and volunteers, NUMA has investigated numerous shipwrecks of historical significance, discovering more than sixty sites from which important artifacts have been removed.

All artifacts have been turned over to the proper authorities for study and conservation. For many years the tale of the *H. L. Hunley* and its fate fascinated NUMA and its founder.

The story of the *Hunley* had never died. Newspaper articles about the boat appeared from time to time. William Alexander, a member of the *Hunley* crew and friend of George Dixon, survived the war and later wrote about the construction and deployment of the boat. P. T. Barnum offered a prize of $100,000 for the remains of the boat so he could exhibit it in his museum. Cussler, a longtime student of the Civil War, was one of many when he decided to try his hand at discovering the resting place of the long-lost submarine. In 1980 Cussler made his first trip to Charleston, the first of many trips, as the search developed and spread across the years.

Over the years NUMA pursued other goals in addition to the search for *Hunley,* and Cussler wrote lots of books. Attempts to locate the lost submarine were often hampered by bad weather, accidents, and incompetent volunteers, and produced many disappointments. But even negative information has some value; it could be said that *Hunley* was definitely *not* in certain well-searched areas. On May 3, 1995, persistence, skill, research, and some good luck paid off. Harry Percorelli, working for NUMA, dove off the *Diversity,* the team's work boat, and laid his hand on the hull of the *H. L. Hunley.* He was soon joined by Wes Hall, another experienced diver. The location was marked, *Hunley* had been found.

This was just the beginning of a long process of deciding what to do with the discovery—should the submarine be left where it was? Should underwater archaeology be done to retrieve artifacts? Should the *Hunley* be raised and preserved?

CHAPTER 10

Now came a mystery of a different kind. Who owned the
wreck? At first, the United States government claimed the right
of possession as "spoils of war." At the end of the Civil War all
surviving property of the Confederate States government—for
example, weapons—was turned over to the US authorities. It was
pointed out that *Hunley* did not belong to the Confederate government; the boat belonged to a group of investors who operated
under a license from the Confederate authorities and who would
be awarded a cash prize if they sank an enemy ship. For this reason
the boat had never been commissioned as the CSS *Hunley* but was
properly referred to as simply the *H. L. Hunley.*

The State of South Carolina felt it had a claim to ownership.
The resting place of *Hunley* was within three miles of the seaward
end of the breakwater that protected the entrance to Charleston
Harbor. This could be held to mean *Hunley* was within the state
jurisdiction. But South Carolina had no plans in hand to protect
the site or to conserve the vessel if it were raised.

NUMA and Clive Cussler were not interested in owning
Hunley, but it was their firmly held opinion that this was too
valuable an artifact not to be studied, learned from, and preserved.
Without the assurance that this would be done, the location
of *Hunley* would remain secret. Eventually a plan of action was
reached, and all the major parties agreed to it.

The State of South Carolina created the *Hunley* Commission to acquire, recover, and preserve the submarine for study by
historians and those interested in the development of submarine
technology. State Senator Glen McConnell became head of the
commission. The commission then formed a not-for-profit group,

the Friends of the *Hunley,* to raise funds to assist in the conservation and eventual display of the boat. It was also agreed that the boat would be raised and taken to the Warren Lasch Conservation Center, an affiliate of Clemson University, for preservation.

The engineering technique to be used to raise *Hunley* presented another challenge. After exposure to salt water for a century and a third, the iron hull would be very fragile. It would not be suitable simply to run slings around the boat and heave away. Finally a system was designed to attach to the hull rubber bags filled with foam to provide buoyancy. The hull could then be surrounded with a supporting cage and brought to the surface. Aboard a barge and while bound for the Lasch Conservation Center, the hull would be sprayed constantly with salt water to retard corrosion.

In August 2000 plans became a reality. *Hunley* was raised and taken to the conservation center. There she has been for eighteen years while the tedious and time-consuming process of excavating the sediment from inside the boat went on and the process of conserving the hull has proceeded.

Inside the center, immersed in a custom-built tank and under constant treatment to stabilize the iron plates of which it is constructed, *Hunley* had the sand and sediment of 130 years removed. In the process other mysteries appeared and were solved.

Ever since the Civil War there had been a romantic tale told about George Dixon and a coin given him by his fiancée, Miss Queenie Bennett. Before Dixon left for the war, Miss Bennett gave him a twenty dollar gold piece. The coin was in Dixon's pocket when he went into combat at Shiloh, Tennessee, on April 6, 1862. During the fighting a rifle slug came screeching through the air and struck Dixon in the thigh, knocking him down. When he tried to stand, he found he was uninjured except for a bruise. The gold piece had stopped the bullet, leaving the coin bent. Dixon had the coin engraved "Shiloh, April 6, 1862. My life preserver. GED" This sounded like a good, romantic, Southern tale of the Civil War.

On May 23, 2001, the remains of the person occupying the command and control position in the crew compartment of the *Hunley* were removed, embedded in a large block of mud and sediment. Archaeologist Maria Jackson was in charge of separating the bones from the mud. Gingerly feeling her way under the left side of the pelvic bone, the scientist let out a gasp. Slowly withdrawing her clenched fist, she opened her palm to reveal Dixon's gift from Queenie Bennett, the engraved gold coin. The romantic story is true.

Another mystery was the discovery of a copper disk engraved with the name of Ezra Chamberlain, Private, Co. K, Seventh Connecticut Infantry. What was this Union soldier doing aboard *Hunley*? Was he a deserter, had he changed sides? Investigation of the service records showed that Chamberlain had been killed in action on July 11, 1863, in an attack on the Confederate-held position called Fort Wagner. The explanation for this mystery is that a Confederate picked up the disk as a battlefield souvenir and later joined the crew of the submarine.

The *Hunley* sank three times and was recovered each time. Each time she went down, the crew was killed. The first two crews had received proper funerals. On April 17, 2004, the remains of the third crew of the *Hunley* were carried to Magnolia Cemetery in Charleston, the final resting place of the two earlier crews.

Thousands of Confederate reenactors marched in solemn procession to accompany the remains. George Dixon and his men were buried in the same plot as H. L. Hunley and those who perished with him.

But the biggest mystery remained. What caused the *H. L. Hunley* to sink? One hatch cover was found to be missing a locking mechanism. Did the boat sail without being watertight? Was the locking mechanism lost when the crew tried to open the hatch to escape? A small, two-inch porthole was found to have its glass broken. Did a rifle shot from USS *Housatonic* hit this vulnerable spot and let water in to sink its attacker? Was the glass broken while the submarine lay a wreck on the sea floor?

Each year since 2000, when the *Hunley* was raised, a memorial service is held on February 17, the night of her successful attack followed by her sinking. At the service in 2010 it was noted that the biggest question of all was still unanswered. Now, however, a possible answer has been provided, an answer that fits the circumstances of the attack of the Hunley on the Housatonic. Ever since the submarine was raised, scientists and historians have been puzzled by the fact that the remains of the crew were found at their action stations, indicating there was no sign of panic or distress. The hull of the vessel had not suffered any obvious damage, so how had the crew met their end? The answer probably is they killed themselves by accident. Researchers from Duke University have conducted tests that point to the weapon carried by the submarine. The "torpedo" carried by the Hunley was a keg containing 135 pounds of gunpowder mounted at the end of a sixteen-foot pole. Detonation of that much gunpowder at that distance from the Hunley would have created a shock wave that would have ruptured the blood vessels in the lungs and brains of the men aboard, killing them instantly. Because of the limits of scientific knowledge at the time of the Civil War, the first submarine carried the source of its own destruction.

Note: Monday through Friday the Lasch Conservation Center is a working laboratory. On Saturday and Sunday the facility is open for tours and the *Hunley* can be viewed in its tank. When the conservation process is completed, the boat and its associated artifacts will go on display in a museum in North Charleston, South Carolina.

CHAPTER 11

Bedecked with a Bonnet in Baltimore

Fearful for his life because of a well-organized plot led by a large number of secessionist-minded Marylanders, president-elect Abraham Lincoln was hesitant to travel through Baltimore while on his way to Washington for his inauguration. Yet, there was no way to bypass the dangers of the hostile city unless Lincoln abandoned his announced schedule and gave up train travel for a carriage or a boat.

Making the best of a bad situation, the newly elected president arranged to arrive in Baltimore in the dead of night. Donning a disguise of a Scotch bonnet and long cloak, Lincoln crept through the streets until reaching the safety of a train on the Washington side of town. Only this extreme caution and lack of boldness preserved his life, although it did call into question his manhood, dignity, and sense of honor. Lincoln may even have worn a dress, disguising himself as a woman. Or, he may have hidden in a cattle car wearing only his nightshirt. At least, so say various legends and tales.

Of all the US presidents, Lincoln has more legends clustering about him than any other. The account of how Abraham Lincoln passed through Baltimore in February 1861 while on his way to Washington to assume office has given birth to one of these legends, one that persists to the present day. Is there any truth to the story of Lincoln being bedecked in a bonnet in Baltimore? Was there any reason to don a disguise? Was Lincoln in danger? Was there a plot to assassinate the president-elect?

It is difficult for people today to envision the feelings of Americans in 1861, so far as Abraham Lincoln is concerned. Today, Lincoln is widely admired and is viewed as a great patriotic leader who preserved the Union and ended slavery in this nation. For most Americans today Lincoln is a beloved figure. In 1861 Lincoln was despised, if not hated, by a large part of the population of the United States. It is obvious that there would have been little admiration for Lincoln in the states forming the Confederacy; what is amazing is the open hostility shown Lincoln in the North. During the presidential campaign of 1860, one newspaper editorialized that Lincoln's approach to the problems facing the nation was so dangerous that he should be immediately hanged. That newspaper was published in Springfield, Illinois, Lincoln's hometown.

Lincoln won the election of 1860 with less than 40 percent of the popular vote, the lowest percentage ever to produce a winning candidate. A victory with less than a majority of the votes is possible because of the system of awarding electoral votes in the Electoral College, and other presidents in addition to Lincoln have been "minority" presidents. In both the 2000 election and the 2016 election the winning candidate has received less than 50 percent of the popular vote. However, most major party candidates who have lost the presidency have gotten more votes than Lincoln did in winning the office, even though Lincoln did garner 180 electoral votes.

Lincoln was aided in his Electoral College victory by a split in the Democratic Party and the presence on the ballot in many states of a strong "third party" movement, the Constitutional Union Party. Democrats had split along sectional lines, with the Southern wing nominating John C. Breckenridge. Breckenridge came from Kentucky and was a former vice president of the United States. He carried most of the Southern states, including Maryland, where Lincoln would get only 2.5 percent of the vote. When war broke out, Breckenridge would join the Confederacy.

Northern Democrats put Stephen A. Douglas on the ballot, the man who had defeated Lincoln for the US Senate in the election that featured the Lincoln-Douglas debates. In the presidential election Douglas would carry only the state of Missouri. Douglas would die of natural causes in 1861.

Lincoln was nominated by the new Republican Party, a political union of former Whigs, Free-Soil supporters, and anti-slavery Democrats. Lincoln's name did not appear on the ballot in every state. Then and now, a candidate does not get a spot on the ballot merely by announcing for the presidency; they must be nominated by a specified number of voters in each state. In some states in 1860, there was no Republican Party organization to collect signatures to get Lincoln on the ballot.

Finally, there was the Constitutional Union Party. As the old Whig Party of Henry Clay and Daniel Webster broke up, many of its members became Republicans. Lincoln himself was an old

Whig. Other former Whigs were not comfortable with the Republican position opposing expansion of slavery into the territories. These old Whigs pointed out that, like it or not, the Supreme Court had ruled in the *Dred Scott* case that all territories were required by law to be open to slavery. Only when a territory became a state, the court had said, could a decision opposing slavery be made.

The Republican position, these old Whigs pointed out, was a radical one that called for actions that were in violation of the law of the land. The only thing to do was to work within the system of laws to either pass a constitutional amendment outlawing the expansion of slavery or get a new justice or two on the Supreme Court and have the issue retried. The motto of the Constitutional Union Party was "The Constitution as it is, the Union as it was." In short, accept slavery since it is protected by the Constitution and keep the Union intact. This party nominated John Bell of Tennessee, a US senator who opposed the idea of leaving the Union. John Bell carried Tennessee, Kentucky, and Virginia. When the war did come, he returned to his home state and went into manufacturing. He died in 1869.

Lincoln came into the presidency in a confusing and controversial election. By the time he was on his way to Washington, seven Southern states had declared themselves out of the Union and were meeting in Montgomery, Alabama, to write a constitution for a new government, the Confederate States of America. Jefferson Davis was soon to be inaugurated president of this new nation. It was under these circumstances that Lincoln began his journey from Springfield to Washington, a journey that would take him through Maryland. Could he make the trip safely?

Complicating Lincoln's travel plans was the nature of railroad travel at that time. Lincoln had planned a twelve-day tour of appearances and speeches to take him from his home to Washington. His intended route would carry him across Illinois, Ohio, Pennsylvania, New York, and then to Baltimore. Passing through Baltimore was a matter of necessity. There were only two rail links between Washington and the Northern states. One ran west from the capital along the Potomac River to Wheeling, Virginia, and then followed the valley of the Ohio River. This was the Baltimore and Ohio Railroad. A second route ran farther north, through Pittsburgh and Philadelphia, branched into New York, and then passed through Wilmington to reach Baltimore.

The first route, the western stretch of the Baltimore and Ohio Railroad, would not take Lincoln to any large cities in states he had won in the election, and it would cause him to traverse parts of Virginia and Maryland. The second route would allow Lincoln to greet those who had supported him and allow him to arouse their enthusiasm for his programs, but the leg of the trip through Baltimore would be tricky. Lincoln, and all other travelers, would arrive at the Calvert Street Station of the Philadelphia, Wilmington, and Baltimore Railroad. From there Lincoln could go by city streets to the Camden Street Station of the Baltimore and Ohio Railroad, or he could stay aboard his railcar while the engine was disconnected, horses hitched to the carriage, and it was towed the mile and a half to the Camden Street Station. Engines were not permitted to run on the tracks that led through the busy heart of Baltimore; they were too loud and too disruptive for the citizens of the day.

The plans made by Lincoln and his entourage were not secret; indeed, the plans had been published in numerous newspapers since the purpose of the trip was to meet supporters and to rally political support. Baltimore city officials knew Lincoln was on his way, but they had made no plans for an official reception, the only city to so respond. This lack of an official welcome raised the question as to whether or not the officials had any plans to protect the president-elect from any potential danger. If local officials were not concerned about Lincoln's safety, then the matter might well be ignored.

At the time of Lincoln's election there was no Secret Service, no Federal Bureau of Investigation. No one had the daily and direct duty of protecting the president. Federal marshals did exist, but they were charged with enforcing federal laws and not with being bodyguards. Also, the president was not perceived to be in danger, as no president had ever been assassinated, and only one assassination attempt had ever been made. A disappointed office-seeker had attacked Andrew Jackson, and "Old Hickory" had knocked the man to the ground with his walking stick. Lincoln was facing an unexpected and unprecedented situation.

The people close to Lincoln had responded to the perception of danger by hiring Allan Pinkerton as a combination information gatherer, secret service operative, and bodyguard. Pinkerton was a forty-two-year-old native of Scotland who had been in the United States since 1842. In Scotland he had been a supporter of the Chartist Movement that advocated universal adult suffrage. In the States his radical political views drew him to the abolitionist movement. He even went to the extreme of assisting runaway slaves and had some association with John Brown. In the early 1850s he founded a detective agency that bore his name. He was successful in solving some railroad robberies, and this success brought him to the attention of an attorney who represented the railroads, Abraham Lincoln.

Pinkerton's ties with the railroads had led him to develop a network of detective company employees in most rail centers, and these now became a source of political news and gossip for the Lincoln party. Some of these detectives reported talk among certain elements in Baltimore that violence might be used to prevent Lincoln from reaching Washington. Pinkerton took this talk seriously, and he convinced those around Lincoln to do the same. Pinkerton and his agents would be around Lincoln, sometimes as obvious members of the party and sometimes blending into the background, but they would provide some degree of protection should violence be attempted against the president-elect.

Another layer of protection would be provided by Ward Hill Lamon, Lincoln's former law partner. Lamon was a native of Virginia who had moved to Illinois in 1847. Like Lincoln, he was not in favor of immediate abolition of slavery, and he had won Lincoln's undying gratitude for packing the hall with moderates at the 1860 Republican convention, keeping the extreme abolitionists away from the proceedings. Lamon had become a prosecuting attorney for the Eighth Judicial District in 1857 but had left his law practice to become Lincoln's self-appointed bodyguard during the presidential campaign. Soon Lincoln would appoint Lamon US marshal for the District of Columbia, and the two would remain close associates for the rest of Lincoln's life. Lamon felt that Lincoln should arm himself for self-defense. Pinkerton felt it would be unseemly for the president to carry weapons. So, Lincoln had two sets of bodyguards but they did not agree on how best to do their job.

As Lincoln traveled to town after town, speaking to his supporters, Pinkerton suggested a change of plans. The speeches were not being greeted with enthusiasm. One commentator said that Lincoln was making a fool of himself and that he was mortifying and shaming the intelligent people of the entire nation. It was as inconceivable, it was said, that Lincoln could become a statesman as it was that a braying donkey could become a noble lion. In the face of disappointing public reaction, the detective wanted Lincoln to cancel some of his stops and make an unexpected dash for Washington. Lincoln felt he needed to keep to his basic schedule, especially to make an appearance at Independence Hall in Philadelphia and to make an address to the Pennsylvania legislature at Harrisburg. After much discussion a compromise was reached.

George Washington's birthday was, in 1861, a major national holiday observed with patriotic gatherings, fireworks, and parades. On February 22 Lincoln made his talk in Harrisburg to the Pennsylvania lawmakers. Pleading fatigue, he returned to his hotel and changed into traveling clothes and an overcoat topped with a soft wool felt hat. Leaving the hotel by a side door, Lincoln and Lamon went to the depot, where an engine hitched to a single passenger car awaited them. Off they sped to Philadelphia. The last train for Baltimore had been kept waiting, with the railroad telling the passengers that important papers for Washington were on the way and that the papers had to be delivered the following morning. When Lincoln's special train arrived, the presidential party quietly boarded the last car of the train, a sleeping car. Pinkerton and some of his detectives were already aboard. Lincoln went into his berth while Lamon and Pinkerton took station outside his door.

The train arrived in Baltimore at three in the morning, was transferred by horses across town, and arrived in Washington at 6:00 a.m. Lincoln was escorted to the Willard Hotel, where rooms were awaiting him. The next day newspapers across the nation erupted with humiliating, scornful articles. The friendly *New York Times* said the episode called into question Lincoln's manhood and implied that a fearful Lincoln had been convinced to continue his trip only at the insistence of his wife and several others. The article in the *Times* included an account of Lincoln being dressed in "a Scotch bonnet and a long cloak" while sneaking through the streets of Baltimore.

Within a few days *Harper's Weekly* turned a verbal account of Lincoln into a picture that showed a grotesque figure dashing in blind panic toward the distant Capitol building. *Vanity Fair* ran a cartoon showing Lincoln disguised in a dress taken from his wife's travel trunk. The *New York Tribune* wrote: "It is the only instance recorded in our history in which the recognized head of a nation has been compelled, for fear of his life, to enter the capital in disguise." The *Baltimore Sun* was much blunter: "Had we any respect for Mr. Lincoln, official or personal, as a man, or as President-elect of the United States, the escapade by which he reached the capital would have utterly demolished it." Within days Lincoln was being ridiculed from coast to coast. The innuendoes about his actions would continue for the rest of his life.

Did Lincoln disguise himself to travel through the unfriendly town of Baltimore? No. Instead of the formal clothes and top hat that became associated with Lincoln in the public mind, he had worn something like a modern business suit and a felt hat. This is what most men of the day wore when traveling; it is what Lincoln wore on many days. One item does deserve mention. Heating was not as efficient then as now, and train cars were somewhat drafty. It was not unusual for men to carry a shawl to drape around their shoulders to protect them from drafts. Lincoln frequently draped a shawl over his shoulders when seated, as did many other men. This may be the origin of the rumor that Lincoln disguised himself as a woman.

Was Baltimore a dangerous place for Lincoln? Certainly he was not popular there nor was he liked in much of the rest of the state of Maryland. On April 19, 1861, just weeks after Lincoln passed through Baltimore in the small hours, a riot occurred when the Sixth Massachusetts Infantry Regiment attempted to march across town between the two train stations. This riot occurred in full daylight and cost the lives of both soldiers and civilians. It should be noted that April 19 was a day of significance in 1861; it was the anniversary of the beginning of the Revolutionary War, the first shots of that conflict having been fired on April 19, 1775.

During the spring of 1861 the fear that Maryland might secede became so intense that Lincoln suspended the writ of habeas corpus throughout the entire state, asserting that the president had the right to hold people in jail without bringing charges against them. By the end of the Civil War, Lincoln had ordered the arrest of 2,094 citizens of Maryland because their political opinions were considered dangerous. This number included twenty-nine members of the state legislature and seventeen owners of newspapers.

Clearly, Lincoln felt that Baltimore and the state of Maryland represented a significant degree of danger.

Was there a conspiracy to assassinate Lincoln? Pinkerton thought so. He was convinced that his agents in Baltimore had uncovered a conspiracy in which at least eight people had each agreed to make an attempt on Lincoln's life. The basis for Pinkerton's belief was laid out in a June 1868 article in *Harper's New Monthly Magazine*. In the article frequent references are made to "Southern fire-eaters" and "beautiful aristocratic belles" who mouthed anti-Lincoln sentiments, but only one name alleged to be involved in a plot is given. This was Cipriano Ferrandini, a thirty-eight-year-old Corsican immigrant who owned a barber shop in the Barnum's Hotel in Baltimore. No indictment was ever made of Mr. Ferrandini nor was anyone else ever arrested on charges associated with a plot. As recently as 2008 a book, *The Baltimore Plot*, revisited the matter and concluded that there was a conspiracy to kill Lincoln and that the danger had been real.

Ward Hill Lamon, in his book on the life of Lincoln, argued that there was no plot. Instead of there being a hundred or so conspirators, he said, there were not even three. Lamon felt a bold front by Lincoln and himself would have seen them safely through Baltimore, that they would have met no opposition, and that Lincoln would have been spared much subsequent embarrassment.

Is there an answer to this mystery? Probably not. But one thing is sure: By going through Baltimore in the dark, early hours instead of proceeding in broad daylight, Lincoln created the conditions that have perpetuated the legend of the president bedecked with a bonnet in Baltimore.

Legends and Myths Shroud the Body of John Wilkes Booth

W ho is buried in the grave of John Wilkes Booth? No, this is not a trick question. The assassination of Abraham Lincoln is one of the most heinous murders in the history of the United States, and the name of John Wilkes Booth is the best known of all such criminals. Yet even to this day, legends and myths surround the question of who is buried in Booth's grave. Was Booth caught? Was he the man killed in a barn in Port Royal, Virginia? Did someone else die in that barn, and did Booth live into the twentieth century? Legends and myths have supported these questions since 1865.

Who was John Wilkes Booth? Booth was the son and brother of famous Shakespearean actors. His father, Junius Brutus Booth Sr., immigrated from Great Britain to the United States and settled in Baltimore. The family also owned a summer cottage near Bel Air, Maryland. Three sons and a daughter were born at this home: Edwin, John Wilkes, Junius Brutus Jr, and Asia. The three sons all became famous actors.

Following his school years, John Wilkes became a professional actor in 1855 at age seventeen. His enthusiasm and energy soon made him a popular performer and he traveled all over the eastern United States appearing in plays. Booth came to be known as "the most handsome man in America"—standing five feet, eight inches tall and weighing 160 pounds, with jet-black hair and beard, he was muscular and had a deep, resonant voice. His only public venture into politics was to endorse a congressional candidate for the anti-immigrant Know-Nothing Party. When the Civil War started, Booth publicly said he considered secession "heroic" but he made no effort to go south to support the Confederacy. The other members of the family were firmly pro-Union.

For reasons not fully known, in the closing months of the war Booth gathered around him a small group of conspirators to form a plot to kidnap President Lincoln, take him behind Confederate lines, and use him as a bargaining chip to negotiate an end to the war that would be acceptable to the South. With the surrender of Robert E. Lee's Army of Northern Virginia on April 9, 1865, the kidnapping plot obviously was not practical, so Booth turned his thoughts to murder.

The known conspirators included John Surrat, a college-educated young man who was a member of the Confederate Secret Service and traveled throughout the North and into Canada promoting the Southern cause; David Herold, a pharmacy clerk who was mentally challenged and who had never served in the Confederate army but had worked in Washington throughout the war; George Azterodt, a German immigrant who had never been in the Confederate army although he had been part of a smuggling operation, slipping people and goods into and out of Confederate territory; Lewis Powell, a Confederate soldier who had been a POW for the last several months of the conflict; and some other people who knew Booth and helped him in a personal way but were not involved in the assassination plot. These included Dr. Samuel Mudd, who treated Booth's broken leg after the assassination, and Mrs. Mary Surrat, at whose boardinghouse the group sometimes met. John Surrat had helped plan the attempt to kidnap Lincoln, but had left Washington for Canada several days before the surrender of Lee on April 9 and thus did not take part in the assassination itself.

On the night of April 14 a comedy, *Our American Cousin,* was playing at Ford's Theatre, a location Booth knew well and where he was well known. The Washington newspapers announced that President and Mrs. Lincoln were to attend the play that night. Booth knew there was a moment during the second act when only one player would be on stage. He planned to strike at that moment and make his escape by jumping to the stage from the box where the presidential party was to be seated. His escape plan was to go back to the area of Maryland he knew so well from his boyhood, the area called the "southern neck," and find a boat to cross the Potomac River. Once in Virginia, Booth thought, he would be received as a hero and would find all the help he needed for whatever the future held.

Booth seems to have spent several hours on April 14 making preparations for his attack on the president and working with his coconspirators to plan attacks on Vice President Andrew Johnson and Secretary of State William Seward. At the chosen moment, Booth struck, firing a bullet from his pistol into the skull of

President Lincoln just behind his left ear. Booth leaped to the stage, catching his spur in the bunting decorating the presidential box and falling in such a way as to break a bone in his left leg. Nevertheless, he was able to make his escape.

Because Booth was a celebrity, several people in the audience at Ford's Theatre recognized him as he made his leap from the presidential box to the stage. Soon his room at a hotel was searched and the manhunt was on. As a wartime security measure, all the bridges and roads leading into and out of Washington were guarded and passage was forbidden after a stated hour. Booth had the good luck, and the smooth tongue, to talk his way past the sentry on the Navy Yard Bridge and rode out of town.

Booth made his escape from Washington and was joined in Maryland by another of the conspirators, David Herold, who had unsuccessfully attacked Secretary Seward. In pain from his broken leg, Booth stopped at the house of Dr. Samuel Mudd, who set the bone and allowed Booth and Herold to spend the rest of the night. This unexpected stop put Booth several hours behind his projected schedule and allowed the authorities to begin their search. Amazingly enough, at first attention did not focus on Booth, despite the testimony of eyewitnesses, because Secretary of War Edwin Stanton thought there was a massive conspiracy to kill all government leaders, a last-ditch attempt by the Confederacy to win the war. Stanton was leading a search for what he thought was a cadre of individuals with a large-scale plot to wipe out the leadership of the government of the United States, and not for a lone assassin. During the day of April 15 Dr. Mudd went to Bryantown, Maryland, on business and learned of the assassination of President Lincoln and of the search for the murderer. Suspecting that his patient might be the wanted man, Dr. Mudd returned home and ordered Booth and Herold off his property. The two men wandered through a swamp until an African American directed them to the house of Samuel Cox, a person Booth knew to be friendly to the South. Cox, however, was unwilling to allow Booth and Herold to stay on his farm and recommended that they hide in a thicket of pine trees until passage across the Potomac River could be arranged.

For five days the two men lived outdoors with no shelter and little food. Booth, who was accustomed to staying at the best hotels and having good food prepared for him, found this existence difficult and the pain from his broken leg only added to his discomfort. On April 22 Booth and Herold, with the aid of Thomas Jones, a Confederate agent, managed to cross the Potomac. Contrary to their expectations, no warm welcome awaited them. Virginians were quite cool toward Booth, barely agreeing to give him food, and then sending him on his way. On April 24 Booth and Herold reached Port Royal and, finding no refuge there, went three miles out into the country toward Bowling Green. There they stopped at the farm of Richard Garrett, who had one son just returned from the Confederate army, and passed themselves off as Southern soldiers from Maryland.On April 25 a patrol from the Sixteenth New York Cavalry reached Port Royal. There they found a man who had traveled for a few hours in company with Booth and Herold and recognized them from pictures he was shown. The patrol was directed to the Garrett farm. This cavalry unit was led by Colonel Everton Conger of the Secret Service and by Lieutenant Luther Baker, nephew of the head of the Secret Service. The cavalrymen arrived at the Garrett farm at two in the morning and the noise of their arrival woke the two sons of the family. They told the patrol that two strangers were sleeping in the barn behind the house.

Colonel Conger had his unit surround the barn and called for the men to come out. After some arguing, Herold came out and surrendered, but Booth refused to leave his refuge. Tired of waiting, Conger set fire to the barn and, as the flames spread, a gunshot was heard. Men rushed into the barn and found Booth dying. Conger had ordered that Booth be taken alive so he could be put on trial. Some eyewitnesses swore that the revolver found near Booth's body had one empty chamber, meaning it had been fired and his death was suicide. However, Sergeant Boston Corbett claimed he fired at Booth, mortally wounding him.

Booth's body was wrapped in a blanket and placed in a wagon to be taken to a wharf on the Potomac River. From there it was taken to the USS *Montauk*, where it lay all day on the deck covered by a tarpaulin. Immediately rumors started, and persist to this day, that the body was not that of John Wilkes Booth.

Some people argued that Secretary of War Edwin Stanton had been involved in a plot to kill Lincoln because he and Lincoln did not agree about the future of the South. Lincoln characterized his plan of reconstruction as "let them up easy," while Stanton and the radical abolitionists wanted to punish the South for rebellion and slavery. With Lincoln dead, the argument went, the radicals could control the agenda. Stanton had conspired with Booth, it was said, to make sure the murder succeeded, but Stanton then made sure Booth was killed so there would be no chance of this arrangement ever becoming public. This conspiracy theory was given additional traction when a diary kept by Booth was handed over to Stanton and later was found to have pages missing. On April 27 Alexander Gardner, a famous photographer, took a picture of the body. Detective James Wardell of the Secret Service took the picture and the glass negative to Secretary Stanton, and it has never been seen since. This was enough to touch off conspiracy theories about whether or not Booth had been killed.

Others argued that Vice President Andrew Johnson had conspired to kill Lincoln because he wanted to be president. Johnson, it was alleged, had helped Booth escape, and someone else who resembled Booth had been killed. Sergeant Corbett was arrested and held for a time because both conspiracy theories held that he had either killed an impostor or had deliberately killed Booth to cover up the plot.

In an attempt to quell these conspiracy rumors, LaFayette Baker, head of the Secret Service, sent some of his staff, a hotel clerk who knew Booth by sight, and Dr. John F. May, who had removed a tumor from Booth's neck some years earlier, to examine the body. The ravages on the body of being on the run for several days, living out-of-doors, and then being left in the sun for a day after his death made their task difficult, but Dr. May positively described the location and position of the scar from his operation and his description matched the marks found on the body. The next day the body was secretly removed from the ship and taken to the Old Penitentiary, a government prison, where it was buried beneath the floor of an unused storeroom. By this time rumors were already circulating that Booth had escaped, and soon there were reports that he had been seen in South America.

John Surrat had not been apprehended when the other conspirators were caught, and fled to Europe. His mother, Mary Surrat, was tried, convicted, and executed for her supposed role in the assassination, becoming the first woman executed by the United States government. John served in the Vatican Zouaves in 1865 and then went to Egypt, where he served briefly in the military forces in that country. He was arrested and extradited to the United States in 1867 and was tried before a civilian court. His trial again fueled speculation about conspiracies that involved government officials and whether or not Booth was the actual villain. His acquittal on all charges only lessened but did not end speculation about Booth.

In 1869 the Booth family received permission to have the remains exhumed and moved to the family burial plot at Green Mount Cemetery in Baltimore, where they were buried in an unmarked plot. At this time Booth's dentist examined the teeth and made a positive identification.

None of this mattered. The rumor that Booth had survived, with or without help from persons unknown in the United States government, persisted. In the early 1870s news spread that John Wilkes Booth was alive and well in Franklin County, Tennessee. This rumor was based on the fact that a J. W. Booth had received a marriage license. In fact, this person was James Wilson Booth, a farmer whose family had lived in the area for over seventy years.

In 1877 Finis L. Bates, an attorney in Granbury, Texas, was summoned to the bedside of John St. Helen, a man with whom he was acquainted. Declaring he was dying, St. Helen said that his real name was John Wilkes Booth, the assassin. St. Helen claimed that Andrew Johnson had conceived a plot to kill Lincoln, recruited

Booth to do the deed, and had given him the password that allowed him to pass the sentries guarding the bridges leading out of Washington. The man who perished in the barn on the Garrett farm had been someone else and was killed solely to allow those involved to collect the reward being offered for Booth. St. Helen also claimed he had wandered around the Western frontier using a number of aliases and keeping a low profile.

St. Helen did not die but recovered and slipped out of town some days later. In 1903 Bates read an article in a Memphis newspaper that recounted the suicide of a drifter in the town of Enid, Oklahoma. This man, calling himself David E. George, had taken poison but had been found before he died. As his last minutes passed, he confessed to one of those attending him that his real name was John Wilkes Booth. A picture of the dead man accompanied the article, and Bates was struck by the resemblance to John St. Helen. Junius Brutus Booth III told reporters that the man strongly resembled his uncle. No one bothered to point out that this identification was made by a man born in 1868, three years after John Wilkes Booth died.

Fascinated by the story, Finis Bates wrote a book, *The Escape and Suicide of John Wilkes Booth*, and got possession of the body, since no relatives had claimed it. To promote his book, and to make additional money, Bates rented out the mummified body to carnival side shows. When Bates died the body was sold to William Evans, the "Carnival King of the Southwest," who continued to tour the corpse. Upon his retirement, Evans took the body to his home in Idaho and put it on display there.

In 1930 another carnival owner, John Harkin, purchased the body and kept it as a side show display. Harkin even assembled a group of medical doctors in Chicago and had them x-ray the remains. This group affirmed that the broken leg and the scar on the neck positively identified the remains as those of John Wilkes Booth. On reading their report, however, one learns that the right leg is identified as "broken just above the ankle." Booth broke his left leg. The mummy continued to be seen at carnivals into the 1950s and seems to have made its last public appearance in the 1970s.

The mummy has, in turn, given rise to its own legend. Every carnival company and every businessman who has owned the artifact is said to have suffered financial disaster and often has come to personal harm.

In 1977 the Federal Bureau of Investigation was allowed to examine the diary kept by Booth during his last days when he was on the run following Lincoln's assassination. Their examination revealed that not only had several pages been removed, but others had been rewritten by someone who forged Booth's handwriting and these forged pages had been carefully bound into the notebook. This touched off another round of conspiracy theories about why Lincoln had been killed, who was behind the act, and whether or not Booth had escaped.

An attempt to settle the question of who is buried in John Wilkes Booth's grave was made in 1994 when a group claiming to be Booth's relatives petitioned the Circuit Court in Baltimore to exhume the body buried in Green Mount Cemetery so DNA tests could be conducted to determine whether or not it was that of John Wilkes Booth. The cemetery trustees opposed this request, and the Circuit Court agreed. In 1996 the Court of Special Appeals upheld this decision.

Who is buried in John Wilkes Booth's grave? Serious historians have no doubt that Booth rests there, but as is so often the case in dealing with the past, myths and legends have a life of their own. Apparently, so does the body of John Wilkes Booth.

Note: George Azterodt, Lewis Powell, David Herold, and Mary Surrat were arrested and tried by a military commission made up of army officers. Found guilty, they were executed by hanging.

Edward Spangler was one of the persons arrested as a conspirator in the assassination plot. He was a carpenter who built scenery at Ford's Theatre, and his only crime was that he held the reigns of Booth's horse when the well-known actor entered the rear door of the playhouse. Sentenced to six years in prison, he was pardoned by President Andrew Johnson in 1865 and lived until 1875.

Dr. Samuel Mudd was tried as a conspirator and escaped hanging by one vote of the panel of military officers hearing the case. Sentenced to life in prison at Dry Tortugas in the Florida Keys, he was released in 1869 after providing medical services to other prisoners during a yellow fever epidemic.

CHAPTER 13

The Strange Civil War Career of Bushrod Johnson

September 20, 1863, almost eleven in the morning; since seven o'clock nine brigades of Confederate troops had been inching through the woods, filtering into position to make a sledge-hammer attack that would shatter the Union lines and allow the Confederate Army of Tennessee to win a clear-cut victory over the Union Army of the Cumberland led by William S. Rosecrans. As the Confederates nervously awaited the order to go forward, the commander of the leading division sat on his horse, surrounded by his staff, ready to coordinate his men and to lead them to victory.

The commander of that division should, by all logic, have never been there. Bushrod Rust Johnson had three good reasons not to be on a battlefield in a gray uniform. One, he was from Ohio and his only child was there even as the hands on the general's watch moved toward 11:00 a.m. Two, Bushrod Johnson had been raised as a Quaker and his parents had tried to inculcate in him principles of peace, but, clearly, he had not become a pacifist. Three,

Johnson came from a family of abolitionists and had once been part of the secret network called the "Underground Railroad." His family was still active in the abolitionist movement even as he sat waiting for the attack to begin. Despite all this, when eleven o'clock came Bushrod Johnson stood up in his stirrups and shouted the command, "Forward, march!"

What strange course of events had brought a man with such a background to such a place?

Johnson was born on October 7, 1817, in Belmont County, Ohio. The family had been in America for at least eighty years, and the original family members seem to have immigrated to escape religious persecution, since the earliest known ancestors were members of the Society of Friends, commonly called the Quakers. Not surprisingly, the immigrants made their way to Pennsylvania, a colony founded to provide a haven for Quakers and other pacifistic groups. Later, descendants migrated to the Shenandoah Valley of Virginia, where they prospered.

With the passing of time the family needed more land, a commodity that became available in the Northwest Territory in the closing years of the eighteenth century. A move to that area would allow the family to acquire more acres and would let them fulfill a religious goal—to live in an area free from slavery. So the Johnson family went to Ohio in 1800, settling on a farm of 640 acres. They were surrounded by a growing community of Quakers, some of whom were attracted by the nascent abolitionist movement. Into this community Bushrod Johnson was born.

The Quaker faith in which Bushrod was raised was quite strict. Distinctive clothing was required so as to avoid ostentatious dress; the pronoun "you" was avoided in favor of "thee"; and activities such as attending militia muster, drinking alcohol, or even taking an oath in court were condemned. Religious services were held at the meetinghouse twice a week, Sunday and Wednesday. Not surprisingly such rigor caused a degree of rebellion among the younger generation, Bushrod among them. In 1835, at the age of eighteen, he enlisted the aid of friends to write to his congressman asking for an appointment to the United States Military Academy at West Point. In March 1836 he was told to report to the academy in the summer.

Life at West Point was not easy for Johnson. He had no background or family attachment to the military, and the discipline there was every bit as strict as that of the Quaker community he had left. Although his scholarly conduct placed him in the top third of his class, his soldierly conduct was lacking and he stood in the lower half of the class in deportment when he graduated. On leaving the academy with his class in 1840, the young officer was assigned to duty at Fort Jesup in Louisiana and then sent to Florida, where he was involved in the campaign against the Seminoles. All this was a far cry from the Quaker atmosphere in which he had been brought up.

Once the Seminoles had been quashed, Johnson was assigned to Jefferson Barracks near St. Louis, a very desirable posting. A round of duty followed at other Western posts until, in 1846, the United States went to war with Mexico. Active duty offered opportunities for promotion; for Johnson it brought professional and personal disaster.

Johnson found himself in the army commanded by General Zachary Taylor, moving across the Rio Grande into northern

Mexico. On May 7, 1846, in Palo Alto, Johnson was part of a 2,200-man force that successfully defended itself against an army of 6,000 Mexican soldiers. On September 19 Johnson was again under fire at Monterrey, where the fighting became house-to-house. In January 1847 he was among the troops who landed from the sea to assault the port city of Veracruz. In all these battles Johnson behaved well, led his men where they were ordered, and did his full duty. Dozens of his fellow officers received promotions, but no rewards came to Johnson. Instead, he was put in charge of a supply base, tasked with sending forward the materials needed by the men going into combat. This was a vital but boring job, far removed from the scene of action and remote from all chances of promotion.

Bored and disgusted with his assignment, Johnson made a major error in judgment, one he certainly knew was wrong. He wrote a letter to a merchant in the United States suggesting that available space on the next supply ship be used to send goods to him. He would sell the goods and divide the profits with the merchant. Making this questionable arrangement an obviously criminal proposal, Johnson suggested that this be done in such a way that the government would pay the cost of shipping. This letter was read by a superior officer, Johnson was called to account for his acts, and he was allowed to resign from the army rather than face court-martial. His reputation and his professional career were in ruins.

Bushrod Johnson had only one resource with which to earn a living—his mind. West Point had provided him with a good education, and now he had to call on that resource to become a teacher. Western Military Institute in Georgetown, Kentucky, had an opening, and Johnson was glad to get the job as a first step toward rehabilitating his life, his reputation, and his finances.

Military academies were growing in popularity, especially in the South where public education was weak if not nonexistent. Thus, most of Johnson's pupils came from the South, and he depended on fostering good relations with them and with their parents. The views of Johnson's early life on pacifism were now gone, and his abolitionist views faced the challenge of where and how to earn a living.

Western Military Institute had a checkered career. Student fees did not cover operating expenses, and the student body was subjected to epidemics of typhoid and cholera, causing the school to close for long periods of time. The school moved several times to new campuses, hoping to find a healthier location that would allow it to attract more students. Slowly matters improved so that in 1852 Johnson found himself co-owner of the school with the faculty rank of colonel and the titles of president and superintendent. His teaching duties included mathematics and engineering.

Ironically, Johnson's co-owner of the institute was Richard Owen, a man with a background in the utopian community of New Harmony, Ohio, and an opponent of slavery. Richard was the son of David Owen, a socialist who attempted to create working communities such as New Harmony in both Europe and the United States. Richard Owen would go on to have a career in geology, serving as state geologist for Indiana, professor at Indiana University, and the first president of Purdue University.

Despite this unusual partnership, it appeared that Johnson's life was taking on a more even keel. This contributed to his decision to get married to Mary Hatch of Georgetown, Kentucky. Now his roots were established in a border state and his ties with Ohio were fraying. The run of good luck was brief, however. By December 1854 classes were suspended because of widespread illness among the cadets. The school never reopened. Just as this financial disaster was occurring, the Johnsons welcomed their first child, Charles Corling Johnson, who proved to be sickly in body and troubled in mind.

In the midst of disaster, opportunity knocked and Johnson and Owen responded by moving their operations to Nashville, Tennessee. They were offered an alliance with the University of Nashville, in which the Western Military Institute would become the literary branch of the university. John Berrien Lindsley had founded the University of Nashville some years earlier, and it was a growing concern. Financial security seemed to be a fact for the Johnson family, and that security had been found in the South. But the fate of Johnson again proved to be star-crossed. No sooner had the school located in Nashville than the student body began to seethe with controversy as national politics became impossible to ignore, particularly the ruling of the Supreme Court in the *Dred Scott* decision, the raid made by John Brown on the United States Arsenal at Harpers Ferry, and the election of 1860.

These same issues caused friction between Johnson and his business partner, Robert Owen. Johnson had become comfortable living in a society in which slaves were present, but the matter bothered Owen. The breaking point between the two came not over this major issue but over their differing philosophies of education. Owen favored an approach in which the students were given broad latitude in exploring subjects and choosing some of the materials to be read and studied. Johnson felt that the rising sectional differences created a demand for more attention to military subjects and more rigid discipline of both mind and body. As a soldier and West Point graduate, Johnson felt he could deliver that kind of education, but Owen felt it would be better to become more flexible. The two men found it best to part, with Johnson buying out Owen's interest in the school.

Just as this business crisis occurred, Johnson lost his wife. With war approaching and the future of the school very much in doubt, Johnson reached a difficult decision about the future of his special-needs son. His conclusion was to go to his family in Ohio. The Republican-abolitionist wing of the family agreed to accept the task of caring for Johnson's son while he returned south, probably to join a Southern army if war came and certainly to train young men for the possible conflict. To guarantee a source of support for his son, Johnson purchased several hundred acres of farmland in Ohio and found renters for the property. Throughout the war Johnson's son would receive income from land owned by a Confederate general and farmed by Union supporters.

Events soon ended the existence of the Western Military Institute as an adjunct of the University of Nashville. All the students left classes to enroll in the forces being raised by the various states, and John Berrien Lindsley, who opposed secession, agreed with Johnson that the establishment should close for the duration. Soon Johnson was an officer in the forces of the State of Tennessee, and when the state left the Union in June 1861, he became a Confederate officer. At this time Johnson was worth just over $17,000 in real estate and personal property in the South and just over $6,000 in Ohio. He was not a slave owner.

During the early days of military preparation, Johnson spent much time using his engineering skills to help lay out defensive works along the Cumberland and Tennessee Rivers and put his old army skills to use drilling the volunteers who wanted to become soldiers. These efforts were rewarded in early 1862 with a promotion to the rank of brigadier general—just in time for Johnson and his new command to be assigned to Fort Donelson.

General Ulysses S. Grant led a Union army against Fort Donelson in February and captured the fort and its garrison. In the fighting that led up to the surrender, Johnson did what was expected of him; he obeyed orders and fought competently. When the Confederates attacked the right flank of the Union line in an attempt to break out of the fort on February 15, Johnson led the way and the attack was entirely successful, but his accomplishments were ignored by his commanding officer so that, instead of escaping, the Southern force returned to the fort. When a conference was held in the Dover Hotel to discuss the situation, Johnson found that a decision to surrender had already been reached, and as two higher ranking officers stated their decision to escape prior to the surrender, Johnson found himself the second in command. He was present when General Simon Bolivar Buckner surrendered Fort Donelson, but he stayed in the background.

The Union success at Fort Donelson produced confusion among the victors almost as much as among the defeated. There were no plans or provisions for dealing with 12,000 or so prisoners. While helping prepare his men for their trip north to hastily

CIVIL WAR MYTHS AND LEGENDS

prepared prison camps, Johnson continued to keep a low profile. On the day the last of his men boarded boats for the north, Johnson simply walked away. No sentry challenged him, so he kept going until he was beyond Union lines. There he found a friendly farmer who loaned him a horse, and Johnson rode off to Nashville, where he rejoined the Confederate forces retreating from Bowling Green, Kentucky. No one ever questioned Johnson's actions aloud, although there were whispers that challenged the propriety of abandoning his men as they went to prison. There were also innuendoes about the dishonorable nature of his act. At any rate, Johnson was back in command of troops at Shiloh in April.

The experienced men Johnson had once commanded were now in prison camps, so the troops he led at Shiloh had never seen battle. This would result in some confusion as the men came under fire for the first time. Also, the senior Confederate generals practiced the bad habit of detaching units without informing the immediate commanders of the men. As a result, as Johnson led his nervous men into combat on April 6, he not only had to exert extra effort to motivate them to move forward, but he suddenly found half his men had been sent on a mission without his knowledge. Seeking to complete his original assignment with only half his manpower, Johnson was hit by a shell fragment and taken to a field hospital.

Again, Johnson had performed capably, but circumstances denied him any chance to distinguish himself. Following Shiloh some officers were promoted to fill the gaps left by death, others were promoted for reasons of merit, but no promotion came to Bushrod Johnson. Weeks passed and the army was again on the move in a strike into Kentucky. This move culminated in the Battle of Perryville, October 7 and 8, 1862.

At Perryville, as he had done at Fort Donelson and at Shiloh, Johnson fought well. His men were properly led; they carried out their orders and achieved their objectives. Nor could anyone question Johnson's personal bravery; he had been in the thick of the fight and had five horses killed under him. Even though the Battle of Perryville brought an end to the Confederate incursion into Kentucky, there followed another round of promotions and honors, and again Bushrod Johnson was overlooked. Was it his Northern origins or his previous association with radical abolitionists, or did his Mexican War reputation still haunt him? For some mysterious reason, Johnson remained a brigadier general.

In November the Confederate army coalesced around Murfreesboro, Tennessee, while the Union forces gathered at Nashville, thirty miles away. In the chilly rains of December, the US forces moved toward the Confederate position. From December 30 to January 1, 1863, fighting raged along the banks of Stones River.

The Confederates began the fight with a surprise attack against the Union right flank. Johnson's command played an important role in this attack. Although the fighting was heavy, Johnson's men pushed back the Union troops and captured a battery of artillery. Through a long day of fighting, Johnson's men advanced more than two miles, displacing the Union line again and again. Then something unexplained happened. A rumor passed along the lines that the brigade had been outflanked and was in danger of being trapped. Suddenly, men who had fought bravely all day began to fall back; then they began to run away.

Johnson rose to the emergency. He galloped his horse to the head of the retreating mass of men, seized a flag from a color bearer, and personally rallied the men. Getting his command back in formation and getting them something to eat used up the remaining daylight. Once more Johnson had done well, but again a twist of fate had ruined his chance of distinction. Instead of ending the day by smashing through the Union line and ensuring victory, Johnson's last act of the day was to halt the retreat of his men.

Johnson's situation comes more sharply into focus when the date is noted carefully. The Emancipation Proclamation was to go into effect on January 1, 1863. On December 30 Bushrod Johnson was leading an attack that came within a few yards of breaking the Union line and severing the line of retreat for the Army of the Cumberland. The destruction of a major US army just hours before the proclamation was issued would have had disastrous political consequences for the Lincoln administration.

On the Confederate side, despite the "what if" nature of the battle, no one had anything but words of praise for Johnson. Even when the men under his command had faltered, he had not. He had gone beyond the expected by rallying his men and leading them back into line. Again, there were rewards and promotions and again none of them came to Bushrod Johnson. The Yankee Quaker felt more and more like an outsider.

An interlude of six months followed Stones River before Johnson was again called to action. Both Union and Confederate armies tried to solve problems of reinforcements, resupply, and sagging morale. In late June 1863 the Union army took the offensive. General William S. Rosecrans sent his Army of the Cumberland south and east in three columns. One of these, led by General George Thomas, advanced through Hoovers Gap. There the US advance was met by Johnson's men. Interestingly, Thomas was a native of Virginia, so North and South found itself commanded by a man who might well have fought on the other side.

The initial Union push through Hoovers Gap was led by John Wilder's brigade of mounted infantry armed with seven-shot Spencer repeating rifles. This force displaced the Confederate cavalry guarding the gap, but Johnson pushed his men forward to seal off the mouth of the gap. For three days, as Union forces steadily grew in number, Johnson did everything right. He kept his men active, alert, and under control, preventing General Thomas from turning the Confederate flank and trapping the Southern army against a flooded river. When the order came to fall back, Johnson could obey it with a good conscience; again he had done his duty. This time good work was rewarded; Johnson was promoted to major general.

So it was that on September 20, 1863, Johnson was at the head of a powerful column of assault. When the order finally came, he gave the command, "Forward." First, at the normal pace of "route step" the dense gray mass moved forward, then at the "quick step" and, finally, the "double quick" followed by the "charge." With the famous Rebel yell rising from thousands of throats, Johnson's attack sailed into a gaping hole in the Union lines, a hole he did not know was there but that he quickly exploited. Again, Johnson did everything right. He kept his men under control, sending units to his right to force additional US troops to retreat; he sent word to the higher command about what had happened so they could react accordingly; and he hit hard and fast when Union troops made a stand. By the end of the day the Confederate Army of Tennessee had won its first clear-cut victory thanks in large part to a pacifist former abolitionist from Ohio.

This was the apex of Johnson's military career. In the late autumn of 1863 he would be part of an unsuccessful Confederate expedition against Knoxville; in 1864 he would be sent to Virginia to help defend Richmond. In Virginia he performed competently until April 5, 1865. As the Confederates abandoned Richmond and fell back, disaster struck Johnson's command at Saylor's Creek. In confused fighting against overwhelming odds, his command fell apart with men surrendering on all sides. This time, unlike at Stones River, Johnson made no appeal to his men to hold on; he escaped capture by running away. As he fled he crossed the path of Robert E. Lee. In a rare display of temper, Lee made it clear to Johnson that his action had been unacceptable and that he should leave the army. Johnson, crushed in spirit, remained with the army but out of sight until the surrender at Appomattox on April 9.

Johnson tried to restart his school in Nashville after the war, but the economic conditions of the Reconstruction era made this impossible. Johnson returned to his home state of Ohio and eked out a living as a farmer. He died on September 12, 1880, and was buried in the cemetery of Miles Station Methodist Church.

The strange career of Bushrod Johnson was still not over. Almost a century after his death, in 1975, with the cooperation of legal and historical authorities in both Ohio and Tennessee, the remains of General Johnson were removed from Miles Station and reburied at the side of his wife in the Old City Cemetery in

Nashville. An appropriate Confederate military marker was placed on the grave in 1990.

Mentally, emotionally, and physically Bushrod Rust Johnson had a strange, even mysterious Civil War career.

Note: Ohio produced a number of Confederate generals in addition to Johnson, including Charles Clark, David Reynolds, Robert Hatton, Phillip N. Luckett, Roswell S. Ripley, and Otho F. Strahl.

CHAPTER 14

The Mystery of the Damage Inside the Turret of USS Monitor

I t is 5:45 p.m., August 5, 2002. Slowly, the turret of the USS *Monitor* breaks the surface of the Atlantic and is lifted aboard the derrick barge *Wotan*. For the first time in 140 years, the USS *Monitor* has its fighting platform above the surface of the water.

The USS *Monitor* sank off Cape Hatteras in a storm on December 31, 1862. Four officers and sixteen seamen went down with the ship; the other members of the crew were rescued by an accompanying vessel. Although the approximate location of the sinking was known, the resting place on the sea-bottom remained something of a mystery, although attempts were made across the years to locate the wreckage.

In August 1973 a group of scientists from Duke University's Marine Laboratory, led by J. G. Newton, was testing geological survey equipment. In testing one of their underwater devices, several contacts suggested the long-lost resting place of *Monitor* had been found. The remains of the famous ironclad lay under 230 feet of water approximately sixteen miles south and east of Cape Hatteras. The excitement generated by this discovery caused the US Naval Academy to get involved along with the US Coast Guard and the National Oceanic and Atmospheric Administration (NOAA). Some artifacts, including a signal lantern and the ship's anchor, were recovered and sent to conservation. A new home was designated for the artifacts: the Mariners' Museum in Newport News, Virginia. This was an appropriate home for the relics since the *Monitor* fought her most famous battle in the waters nearby.

From 1998 to 2001, NOAA, assisted by scientists from several universities, recovered more artifacts from the *Monitor*. These included the nine-foot-long cast-iron propeller, the engines, a thermometer still in working condition, and various small objects. Then came the grand prize—the gun turret.

The most famous vessel to be part of the US Navy during the Civil War had changed the course of naval warfare in its fight with the Confederate armored vessel CSS *Virginia* on March 9, 1862. Of equal importance to the results of the tactical stalemate with *Virginia* were the technological innovations that characterized the *Monitor*: cannon mounted in a revolving gun turret, purpose-built armor plate, and advanced design steam engines. The recovery of *Monitor*'s gun turret, in addition to the salvaging of other artifacts, was a major feat in preserving Civil War history. It also presented students of the war with a mystery.

The *Wotan* barge carried its cargo of history to the Mariners' Museum, where the *Monitor*'s turret was placed in a liquid-filled tank for stabilization. While in the tank a team of archaeologists began to excavate from the interior of the turret tons of sand and silt that had built up over the last fourteen decades. An abundance of artifacts was recovered in this process but, when the turret was about half excavated, the archaeologists uncovered a mystery.

On the inside of the turret, directly opposite the two gun ports, was evidence that heavy objects had impacted the iron plating of the turret walls. This damage had not been inflicted during the battle with the CSS *Virginia*. During that fight, shots from the Confederate vessel had struck *Monitor* repeatedly. Some of those shots had indeed dented the iron armor of the ship, but these dents bulged from the outside in. The mystery damage showed the blow had been struck on the inside of the turret wall, bulging it outward. What could have caused this? A lengthy investigation of all available records was required before an answer could be found for this puzzle.

When the Civil War began, one of the first steps taken by the Lincoln administration was to declare a blockade of all Confederate ports. This would prevent the South from exporting cotton that could be sold in Europe and gaining money used to purchase weapons and supplies for carrying on the war. At the time the blockade was declared, all the oceangoing ships in the US Navy were of wooden construction. Some of these ships had steam engines, but most of those used sail to supplement their steam power, and many of the navy's ships were sail powered only.

The idea of putting armor plates on naval vessels had been discussed since the 1840s. The development of steam engines made it possible to build these heavier ships, but there had been no impetus to try the experiment of armoring ships. The Confederacy now had the impetus to try. If a few armored ships could be constructed, the Confederacy could easily destroy the wooden ships blockading Confederate ports, opening the door for trade with Europe. This trade would certainly bring in materials for the war effort, and it might bring diplomatic recognition of the Confederacy, possible foreign intervention, and victory in the war. This was certainly impetus enough to try armored ships. Stephen Mallory, Confederate secretary of the navy, gave the order to go forward.

Plagued by a scarcity of shipyards in which to build an armored ship, the Confederates tried a shortcut. The US Navy had evacuated Gosport Naval Yard at Norfolk, Virginia, in early 1861. Before leaving, the USS *Merrimack* had been burned, and the hull below the waterline sank. Mallory ordered the hull of *Merrimack* raised, the engines refurbished, and a new wooden casement covered with iron plates to be built above the waterline. Work was soon under way.

The Confederate activity was no secret. The Gosport Naval Yard was open to visitors, and newspapers carried articles about the progress of work on the new armored ship. The certainty that a Confederate ironclad would soon be at sea put pressure on US Secretary of the Navy Gideon Welles to respond. Welles knew the Union had the industrial capacity to build armored ships— they were already being produced. But the ironclads being built belonged to the US Army, not the navy!

On the Ohio and Mississippi Rivers, boatyards had already begun construction of iron-plated gunboats for use on the western rivers. These were used successfully in combat in February 1862 at Fort Henry and Fort Donelson in Tennessee. Welles hoped something bigger and better could be developed for the navy, something capable of functioning on blue water. On August 3, 1861, Welles published a call for proposals, asking marine designers to submit plans for armored, seagoing warships. A committee called the "ironclad board" was established to evaluate designs.

Several designs were submitted to the ironclad board, most of them being variations of traditional hull shapes covered with iron plates. These were very similar to the boats doing service on the western rivers. One man had a bold new design in mind, a plan for something quite different from any ship afloat. John Ericsson submitted plans and a scale model, which so impressed the ironclad board that he was awarded a contract to begin construction.

Ericsson's design called for an underwater hull made of wood. This hull would be 122 feet long and 34 feet wide. Atop this would be an above-water hull 172 feet in length and 42 feet wide. This upper hull would be plated with iron and would overhang the wooden lower hull on all sides. With only eighteen inches of the upper hull above the water line, no wood would be exposed to enemy artillery fire while the armored overhang protected the ship from being rammed. This was only the first unique feature. The anchor could be raised and lowered utilizing an internal well, so that the anchor was not visible on the outside of the ship.

Just behind the anchor well was a rectangular pilothouse, a structure just under four feet in height. The pilothouse was built of bars of wrought iron bolted together with a slit five-eighths of an inch wide, just below the top of the structure, to allow the pilot visibility to steer the ship. Below-deck ventilation was provided by a system of pipes and blowers, since no ports penetrated the armored sides, which, in any case, were only eighteen inches above the water.

The ship was powered by two steam engines that had forced-air blowers to keep the fires burning in the furnaces.

The most striking of Ericsson's unusual design features was a rotating turret, twenty feet in diameter and nine feet high. The sides of the turret were made of eight thicknesses of one-inch iron plates riveted together. The turret rested on a brass ring set into the armored deck and was turned by its own steam engine. The rotating turret was pierced by two gun ports, side by side. These could be closed with iron shutters when the guns were not in use. All other ships carried the major part of their weapons projecting over the side—that is, the guns were mounted broadside. In order to point the guns at a target, it was necessary to turn the entire ship. With Ericsson's rotating turret the guns could be turned, instead of the ship being turned to aim the guns.

And what guns they would be! Ericsson planned for the ship to carry two cannon of the Dahlgren design. These guns were shaped something like a bottle, being much thicker at the breech than they were at the muzzle. The guns actually mounted in the turret were eleven inches in the bore and used fifteen pounds of black powder to fire a shot that weighed 166 pounds. The cannon themselves weighed over 15,000 pounds each.

There was no hydraulic system to cushion the recoil of these guns. The usual method of handling the recoil of guns aboard a ship was to allow the cannon to "kick back" for a distance when it was fired; then ropes attached from the gun to the hull of the ship would stop the recoil. There was not room enough in Ericsson's turret for this traditional method to be utilized, so a braking system was designed and built into the gun carriages.

Ericsson and the US Navy knew they were in a race with the men working on the *Virginia*. To speed up the work, Ericsson drew up eight contracts with eight different foundries, each of whom would create different pieces of his ship. All the components would be shipped to the Continental Iron Works at Greenpoint, New York, where the actual construction would take place.

On January 30, 1862, only 118 days after work began, the ship now named USS *Monitor* was launched. Testing of the machinery revealed that some adjustments needed to be made, but soon the commander of the ship, Lieutenant John Lorimer Worden, was ready to bring aboard an all-volunteer crew. On February 20, 1862, *Monitor* received orders to sail to Hampton Roads. The *Virginia* was said to be almost completed. On March 6, towed by the tug *Seth Low*, the *Monitor*'s journey began. Workmen had been aboard until the last minute.

Stormy weather awaited *Monitor* on March 7. With only eighteen inches of freeboard, waves broke over the flat-armored deck and smashed against the turret. A hemp rope had been packed into the groove where the turret rested on its brass plate, but this did not prove to be a watertight seal. Water also spurted into the interior of the ship through the hawse holes where the chain for the anchor was let in and out.

Some of this water made its way to the engine room and began dripping onto the leather belts that connected the ventilating fans to their drive shafts. The wet leather slowly stretched and slipped so that the fans stopped turning. Almost immediately the temperature in the engine room rose, and smoke and fumes from the boiler fires filled the now-unventilated hull. As crew members began to choke and pass out from the polluted air, frantic signals were made to the *Seth Low*. After some time the conditions were understood aboard the towing ship and *Monitor* was pulled several miles closer to shore, where calmer water was found. This allowed the bilges to be pumped dry and the ventilation system restored.

March 8 saw calmer seas, and *Monitor* sailed past Cape Henry into Chesapeake Bay. Soon after entering the bay, some of the crew called the attention of the officers to the distant sound of cannon fire. *Virginia* had sailed and the iron Goliath was loose amid the wooden Union fleet. The Confederate ship was under the command of an experienced officer who had seen many years' service in the US Navy prior to the Civil War. Captain Franklin Buchanan of Maryland had been in the naval service since 1815, and he had served as the first commandant of the United States Naval Academy, a school that had largely been his idea. Buchanan was a veteran of the war with Mexico and had been an officer in the fleet that had sailed to Japan under the command of Commodore Matthew Perry. Ironically, as commander of the first oceangoing armored ship to enter combat, Buchanan would become a casualty before the end of the day, struck in the thigh by a rifle bullet as he stood atop the casemate of his ship to get a better view of the fighting.

Also aboard *Virginia* was Lieutenant John Mercer Brooke, another former officer of the US Navy. Brooke had designed a new model of naval cannon that bore his name; they were called "Brooke rifles." These were cast-iron guns with rifled bores; the breech of each gun was reinforced with one or more bands of wrought iron so as to allow them to accept heavier charges of gunpowder. Two of Brooke's cannon were aboard *Virginia*.

Now, practically in sight of the enemy, it struck Lieutenant Worden that he had not had time or opportunity to drill his men at the guns. The crew was made up of veteran sailors and the basic actions of loading, firing, swabbing out, and reloading a cannon were familiar to them, but there were some unusual features to *Monitor* and some familiarization with the weapons system was needed. "Battle Stations" was sounded and the gun crews took their places. The first shots fired from the huge Dahlgrens revealed a serious problem, and Worden utilized the only solution he could think of that could be applied on short notice.

On March 9, 1862, *Monitor* sailed into battle. *Virginia* had caused havoc on March 8, damaging and sinking ships. When fighting ceased that day as darkness fell, the USS *Minnesota* was aground and the USS *Congress* was burning. About 7:00 a.m. on March 9, *Virginia* was seen coming back to finish the job. This time *Monitor* was waiting. At 8:45 a.m. the two ironclads fired their first shots at each other. With that sound, the day of the wooden navy was past.

For the next two hours the two ships fired their enormous cannon at each other. At times they were a hundred yards apart; at other times their hulls touched. Each ship scored hit after hit against the other; both suffered some damage. The advantage in the fight swung back and forth. At one time *Virginia* ran aground, allowing *Monitor* to take up a position where none of *Virginia*'s guns could hit it and to fire unopposed. Still, no decisive damage resulted. At another time *Virginia* was able to ram *Monitor,* causing the Union ship to wallow violently from side to side, but the ship regained an even keel.

Finally, as *Monitor* was passing by the stern of *Virginia,* the Southern ship hit the pilothouse on *Monitor* with a shell. The explosion drove fragments of the shell into the narrow slit through which the pilot looked. The blast and some fragments struck Lieutenant Worden in the face, blinding him. At this point, both ships saw fit to break off the fight. Worden would slowly recover his sight and would rise to the rank of rear admiral.

In one sense, the battle was a stalemate. Neither ship had disabled the other. In a larger sense, *Monitor* had won. The blockade remained intact, and Southern ports would stay closed. With a larger industrial base, the North could, and would, produce many copies of Ericsson's ship.

A few weeks later, as the Confederate army fell back from Norfolk, *Virginia* was unable to sail up the shallow James River. The crew blew up the ship. *Monitor* fought one engagement with a Confederate fort but could not force her way past. In December 1862 the ship was ordered south and sank during the voyage.

During the famous battle of March 9, 1862, each ship had scored hits on the other and each had scars to show for its engagement, but neither ship had penetrated the armor of the other. So, what was the cause of the mysterious damage to the inside of *Monitor*'s turret?

Because of the rush to complete the construction of the ship and to make the necessary adjustments to its machinery, there had been no opportunity to drill the crew at their battle stations. Bad weather had prevented such practice on the voyage from New York to Hampton Roads. Only on hearing the sound of *Virginia*'s guns on March 8 was there time for gun drill. While the men knew the basic drill needed to fire the cannon, the guns on *Monitor* were not equipped with the traditional method of handling the recoil. Instead, they were equipped with a braking system unfamiliar to the crew. When the guns were loaded and fired during the drill on March 8, the brakes were improperly set. On discharge, both the mammoth Dahlgren guns recoiled all the way across the turret and slammed into the iron plates of its side, leaving obvious dents. There was no time to seek expert advice on the proper use of the brakes, no time to train the gun crews even if the proper procedure was known. Lieutenant Worden immediately adopted an expedient that solved the problem.

Worden ordered the men in the ship's magazine to make up powder cartridges that contained less than the regulation charge of powder. Knowing the fight would likely be at short range, Worden decided that fifteen pounds of powder would not be needed for shooting at a distant target. A smaller charge would reduce the recoil and prevent *Monitor* from battering herself to pieces. Not a perfect solution, but it worked.

Today, thanks to a careful investigation of the records, the mysterious dents on the inside of *Monitor*'s turret are a reminder of an ingenious solution to an unexpected problem that arose on an innovative warship.

CHAPTER 15

Revenge and Respect:
The Legacy of Arlington Cemetery

As one leaves the visitor center at Arlington National Cemetery, one sees a sign reading:

> Welcome to Arlington National Cemetery, our nation's most sacred shrine. Please conduct yourselves with dignity and respect at all times. Please remember these are hallowed grounds.

Many, if not most, US citizens would probably agree that Arlington Cemetery is America's most sacred shrine. More than 300,000 American servicemen and women are buried here. More than four million people come each year to pay respectful homage to the sacrifices those servicemen made. For many Americans the Tomb of the Unknown Soldier and the Eternal Flame at the grave of President John F. Kennedy are indeed hallowed ground. Arlington, today, is a great symbol of national pride and unity. It has not always been so. The origins of Arlington National Cemetery are marked with a certain spirit of revenge, and the transformation of Arlington into a place of peace and respect is one of the legendary accounts of the Civil War and its aftermath.

John Parke Custis was the son of Martha Washington by her first marriage. Her second husband, George Washington, never became a biological father, so John was adopted by the Father of Our Country. In 1778, while the War for Independence was going on, Custis purchased 1,000 acres of thickly wooded land overlooking the Potomac River. One attraction of the location was that it was below the point where the river passed over falls and rapids— the "fall line"—which ended easy communication with the coast. By being below the fall line, the estate, when it was developed, could ship its produce by water to the port of Alexandria and, hence, to markets throughout the colonies and Europe.

John Parke Custis did not live to see his dream realized. He died of disease in 1781 while serving under his adoptive father, General George Washington, at the siege of Yorktown. John left a family behind, and the youngest of his children, a six-week-old infant named George Washington Parke Custis, was adopted by his grandparents, George and Martha Washington. G. W. P. Custis grew up surrounded by the people and events that shaped our nation, as America won its independence, experimented with being a loosely organized confederacy, and then wrote and ratified the Constitution.

Much beloved, George Washington died in 1799; three years later G. W. P. Custis reached his twenty-first birthday and inherited the land his father had purchased in 1778. Immediately he began developing the estate and building a house there. By this time the house overlooked not swampy fields across the Potomac River but the beginnings of the nation's capital. A decision had been reached to move the center of government from New York City to a more central location. The District of Columbia had been surveyed on the north bank of the Potomac, and the city of Washington was being built. As the house across the river rose, Custis chose the name "Arlington" for his estate because the family had once owned another property by that name.

It took sixteen years to build the main house, which was completed in 1818. During this time Custis married Mary Fitzhugh and purchased a great many things that had belonged to George Washington. Although the couple enjoyed life in their fine home with its impressive setting, they were unfortunate in their family life. Of their many children, only one, Mary Anna Randolph Custis, survived childhood. In 1831 this daughter married a young army officer named Robert Edward Lee. In the autumn of 1857 Mary Custis Lee became the owner of Arlington upon the death of her father. The estate included several large farms totaling over 5,000 acres and 150 slaves. All the slaves were to be emancipated within five years of the probating of the will. The task of administering the provisions of the will fell to Robert E. Lee.

When the Civil War began in April 1861, Mary Custis Lee was at home in Arlington while her husband was performing his military duties in the US Army. When President Abraham Lincoln called for 75,000 troops to "suppress a rebellion" in the deep South states that had formed the Confederate States, Virginia left the Union as well. Robert E. Lee resigned his commission in the

United States Army and went to Richmond to offer his services to his native state. Mary Lee remained in her home at Arlington.

Also in Washington in April 1861 was Montgomery Cunningham Meigs, an engineering officer in the US Army. Meigs was born in Augusta, Georgia, but both his parents were from New England. Meigs's father, Charles, was a physician who had set up a medical practice in Augusta, but he abandoned that business to return north while Montgomery was still a child.

Meigs entered West Point in 1832 and graduated in the top ranks of his class in 1836. Like most of the top graduates of the military academy, he was appointed to the Corps of Engineers. In the early part of his career, he served under Lieutenant Robert E. Lee, who was tasked to improve navigation on the Mississippi River. After several appointments in various parts of the United States, Meigs was assigned to Washington, DC, and was given the responsibility of building an aqueduct from the Great Falls on the Potomac to the city reservoir. Constructing the aqueduct involved building a bridge over Cabin John Creek, a tributary of the Potomac. This bridge was a tremendous feat of engineering, involving the construction of what was, at the time, the longest single-span masonry arch in the world. Meigs also worked on the Capitol building and the post office building. Spending so much of his career designing and constructing the home of the national government only deepened Meigs's attachment to that government.

Just before the outbreak of the Civil War, Meigs became embroiled in a dispute with Secretary of War John B. Floyd. Floyd used his position to assign Meigs to duty at Dry Tortugas and Key West in Florida, two very undesirable posts. A few weeks later

Floyd, having completed his term of office, left for the South to join the Confederacy. Friends in the Lincoln administration then called Meigs back to Washington.

Just as the first shots of the war were being fired in Charleston, South Carolina, when Confederates bombarded Fort Sumter, Meigs was asked to take part in a highly secret mission to send reinforcements to the garrison at Fort Pickens in Pensacola, Florida. Although not so strategic a location as Fort Sumter, the loss of Fort Pickens would be another blow to the prestige of the United States and the morale of the Northern people. The mission was completely successful and was carried out in an efficient manner. One month later Montgomery Meigs was promoted to brigadier general and was made quartermaster general of the United States Army. In this position Meigs would have responsibility for supplying and transporting all US soldiers. The previous quartermaster general, Joseph Johnston, had just resigned to join the Confederacy.

Meigs brought hard work, dedication, and efficiency to his job. He understood that the United States had the manpower, money, and industrial resources needed to win the war, and he had the willingness to use all these things. He also brought to his task an implacable hatred of the Confederacy and of those who supported it. Revenge and spite had a place in his heart.

By the summer of 1861 the Lee house, Arlington, stood vacant. Mary Lee had remained in the house for several weeks until a relative employed in the War Department warned her that the US Army planned to seize the property. The valuables and furniture that could not be removed were packed away and, turning over the keys to a trusted slave woman, Selina Gray, Mary Lee went south.

The 1861 decision to occupy Arlington was purely military. The house sits atop a hill, commanding a sweeping view over all of Washington. Artillery placed on the heights could drive the president out of the White House and Congress out of the Capitol. By midsummer 1861, trees had been felled and dirt had been moved to build a strong earthwork fort, Fort Myer, on the southern-facing slope. Any guns placed on Arlington Heights would have the US flag flying over them!

By 1862 preserving the Union, and that alone, was no longer a sufficient motivation for fighting such a bloody and costly war. Something more was needed to rally public opinion and to prevent European nations from recognizing the Confederacy. President Lincoln opposed slavery, but he had to move cautiously for political reasons—being too bold in opposing slavery would alienate pro-Union slaveholders in Maryland, Kentucky, and Missouri. In most northern states African Americans were not welcome because they were seen as a threat to white workers; black men were willing to accept lower wages. But now the abolitionists were demanding action in return for their support. There was one major problem: the law. The *Dred Scott* decision by the US Supreme Court had ruled that "neither the president nor Congress" could end slavery, that only states had the authority to do so. However, the District of Columbia was not a state, so slavery was abolished there in April 1862. (The *Dred Scott* decision was later overturned by the passage of the Thirteenth Amendment in 1865.)

In September 1862 the Battle of Antietam gave President Lincoln an opportunity to take a larger step. He issued the Emancipation Proclamation, which was to take effect on January 1, 1863.

Any states still in rebellion at that time would lose their slaves as punishment, but if they returned they could keep their slaves. Ironically, all slaves behind Union lines would remain slaves. Space for housing freedmen in Washington was already scarce, and the proclamation was sure to bring many more there.

Montgomery Meigs suggested that the solution to housing the freedmen was to confiscate additional land at Arlington and create a community for the former slaves. The property tax of $90 was due, and a recently passed law required the owner of the property to appear in person to pay the tax. Mary Lee, obviously, could not come to Alexandria to pay the taxes, but she had sent a personal representative, only to see her delegate turned away. Under the pretext of unpaid taxes, Arlington was sold to the United States government and turned over to the Quartermaster Department. Within days "Freedman's Village" was under construction, with control of the housing and residents to be in the hands of General Meigs.

Originally, the village was a collection of fifty duplex houses. Schools for children were built to provide basic literacy education, and job-training schools were developed for adults. Colonel Elias Greene, a Quartermaster Department officer, wrote that putting the freedmen to work as farm laborers, "a healthy vocation in the pure country air," would be good for all concerned.

Unfortunately, life at Arlington in the Freedman's Village was far from idyllic. Most of the men living there were forced to work on government construction projects for which they were paid $10 a week. From this amount $5 was deducted for housing and services. When the women and children could not grow enough food to supplement the men's income, the residents found themselves "free" to go begging on the streets of Washington. Some of the men complained that their freedom was illusory; they had been forced to work in the fields in return for food, clothing, and shelter, and now they were forced to work for the US government and did not receive enough to provide food, clothing, and shelter. In an additional irony, Robert E. Lee fulfilled the requirements of the will of G. W. P. Custis and manumitted all the Arlington slaves in the winter of 1862. Although Freedman's Village outlasted the Civil War by more than twenty years, it never fulfilled the dreams of the freedmen. Confiscating Arlington did give Montgomery Meigs a great deal of satisfaction.

The spring of 1864 brought the Civil War to a turning point. National elections would be held in the fall. War-weariness was evident in many parts of the North. Militarily, the Confederacy could not win, but if public support collapsed, the North could lose. In Georgia the Union armies led by William Sherman slowly slogged their way toward Atlanta; in Virginia Ulysses Grant made very slow progress toward Richmond; all the while the casualty list grew longer and the piles of bodies grew higher. Men killed in battle were buried where they fell, but wounded men who could stand the journey were sent to the rear-area hospitals. Washington was a major center for medical care for Union wounded, and hundreds of men made the journey to hospitals there only to succumb to their wounds. If a family could pay for the services, the body of the deceased soldier would be embalmed and sent home. If not, the government would take care of the burial, but not in a very elaborate fashion.

CHAPTER 15

Among the many other duties that came his way, Montgomery Meigs was in charge of burying the dead, and his eyes, not surprisingly, fell on the remaining broad fields of Arlington. On May 13, 1864, Private William Christman, Sixty-Seventh Pennsylvania Infantry, became the first soldier to be buried in the soil of Arlington. Private Christman did not die a hero's death on the battlefield; indeed, he never saw combat. He died of illness. Soon there were numerous graves adjoining his—those for indigent soldiers who were buried just across a narrow lane from the slaves who had died over the years at Arlington, and those who had more recently died from Freedman's Village.

Having made a de facto cemetery of Arlington, Meigs decided he should seek approval for his actions. On June 15, 1864, he wrote Secretary of War Edwin Stanton for approval to make Arlington a national military cemetery. Stanton immediately approved the proposal. Shortly after making these arrangements, Meigs visited Arlington. To his anger and disgust, he found that the Union dead were being buried at some distance from the house itself. The officers who had offices and quarters in the house did not want the graves too close to them. Meigs sent the officers to other quarters, installed men who shared his point of view, and ordered bodies buried in the flower garden where the Lees had once relaxed in the cool of the evening.

This determination to get revenge on Lee, and on all Confederates, by making the house uninhabitable was exacerbated by the death of Meigs's son on October 3, 1864. Meigs made it a personal crusade to have the bodies of Union soldiers buried as close to Arlington house as possible. At the end of the war, Meigs was one of the shrill voices who called for the execution or exile of all Confederate leaders, a point of view completely at odds with that of President Lincoln.

With the end of the war, Arlington was now a national military cemetery in practice, but was it in law? Robert E. Lee had his attorney investigate the matter, but the legal question was never raised when Lee died in 1870. A request to Congress from Mary Lee to return the estate was coldly rebuffed. Five months before her death in 1873, she paid a farewell visit to the house. Montgomery Meigs, still in charge of the cemetery, was busily adding to his transformation of the place.

In 1874 Custis Lee, oldest son of General Lee, filed a petition in Congress asking for an admission that the Arlington property had been taken without due process of law. Meigs opposed the petition, and it died without ever being debated. Custis, like his father, knew the value of an offensive move. In 1877 Rutherford B. Hayes, a Union veteran, was elected president on a promise to reunify North and South. Reconstruction, Hayes said, was over and a time for reconciliation had come. Custis Lee filed suit in Alexandria, Virginia, for the return of Arlington. The US government asked for the case to be sent to a federal court and it was. On January 30, 1879, the federal jury found in favor of Lee. On appeal, the US Supreme Court upheld the jury decision on December 4, 1882. That same year Montgomery Meigs retired from the US Army.

The Lee family once again owned Arlington. Legally, the US Army post of Fort Myer, the residents of Freedman's Village, and the 20,000 bodies buried on the property were all trespassers. Custis Lee had the backing of the US Supreme Court if he wanted to take a hard line and reclaim the Arlington property. Instead, in a gesture that recognized both the realities of the situation and that embodied a desire for healing old wounds, Lee offered to sell Arlington at a fair market price. On March 31, 1883, the oldest son of Robert E. Lee went to the office of the secretary of war, an office then held by Robert Todd Lincoln, oldest son of Abraham Lincoln, to receive a check for Arlington. This symbolic meeting of the two families most closely associated in the public mind with the war was taken as a gesture to be followed by others.

Revenge and spite were receding, peace and respect were advancing. But two mysterious twists were still to unfold in the Arlington story. The land comprising Arlington National Cemetery was now under the control of the United States Army. The land was desired by the army for several purposes, and one area was considered an eyesore, given over to an inappropriate use. That area was Freedman's Village. On December 7, 1887, not quite twenty-five years after President Lincoln issued the Emancipation Proclamation, the residents of the village were given a notice of eviction. The army that had made freedom from slavery one of its goals now drove from their homes the people they had freed.

In 1898 the United States went to war with Spain. Many young men from the South enlisted in the United States Army; indeed, one Confederate general, Joseph Wheeler, reentered the service. In a further gesture toward national reunification, President William McKinley proposed that the US government should begin to care for the graves of Confederates buried in the North, many of them men who had died in hospitals or in prisoner of war camps.

By 1900 the remains of Confederates who had been buried in several small plots around Washington had been moved to Arlington. In 1906 a Confederate monument began to be planned, and in 1914 a bronze sculpture by Moses Ezekiel was dedicated in a ceremony led by President Woodrow Wilson. As a young boy attending the Virginia Military Institute, Moses Ezekiel had fought in the Battle of New Market in 1864. At the dedication, aging Confederate veterans were joined by equally old Union veterans. Respect, each for the other, had replaced revenge.

Today Arlington is indeed a place of peace and respect. The atmosphere maintained there has an aura of the sacred about it. But the past of Arlington is as mysterious and troubled as the war that made it into a cemetery.

The Mythic, Legendary, Elusive, Mysterious Ku Klux Klan

KK, the Klan, Ku Klux—these words have sent a shiver along the spine of generations of Americans ever since 1866 when the organization was founded. The words call up images of white-robed figures on horseback, galloping through the night; of fiery crosses burning in public places; of beatings, assaults, intimidation, and murder. There is an impression that the Klan was a vast, well-organized movement across the postwar South, with all its activities coordinated by a man with the sinister title of "Grand Wizard," a title held by former Confederate general Nathan Bedford Forrest.

Such is the popular image. But, how much of this is history and how much is myth? This difficult question deserves careful investigation.

It is a historical fact that the Ku Klux Klan began in December 1865 in Pulaski, Tennessee, when six young men, all Confederate veterans, became bored with the routine life of a small town.

These men—John C. Lester, John B. Kennedy, James R. Crowe, Frank O. McCord, Richard R. Reed, and J. Calvin Jones—decided to form a club and engage in some pranks to enliven the dull days. Their objective was, at this point, strictly amusement.

Drawing on their knowledge of the classics and of Greek myths, the members came up with weird and grotesque names for the officers of their new club. They decided to call their meeting place a "den" and the head of the group would be styled the "Grand Cyclops." The members who held no office were to be known as "Ghouls." At first, there were more officers than there were members. They decided on a name that used alliteration but which also drew on the tradition of Greek fraternal organizations. In Greek fraternities the word kuklos is frequently used since it means "circle," implying a band of brothers. The incipient group decided to split the Greek kuklos into two words, which they spelled Ku Klux. The word "clan" was suggested but with a spelling change to make it Klan.

One form of entertainment pursued by the group was to dress up in costumes and parade through Pulaski and some of the surrounding villages. Accounts of these parades, from 1866 and 1867, depict participants dressed in a wide variety of costumes, including women's dresses, riding in lines that wove in and out of town streets so that each rider passed the same point several times. The largest of these parades, held on July 4, 1866, consisted of seventy-five riders. All the newspaper descriptions of these parades are written in the exaggerated, "tall tale" tradition that was a staple of journalism at the time. The early parades were theatrical rather than political in focus, but this would change.

At the end of the Civil War there were many unanswered questions that had been raised by the conflict, but none was more important than deciding what would be the fate of the "freedmen." The Thirteenth Amendment to the Constitution ended slavery but it did not address the question of "what now?" African Americans were free, but what did that mean? Were they free to live in the United States as residents? Were they citizens? Did freedom mean equality? These questions were not fully addressed by either President Lincoln or Congress during the war years. It was clear that Lincoln favored a quick and easy return to the Union by the seceded states because his goal was always to preserve and protect the Union. Ending slavery became part of the means to that end. The abolitionist wing of the Republicans pursued a broader goal: They wanted an end to slavery that would be followed by the creation of a society based on racial equality with equal civil rights guaranteed by amendments to the Constitution.

Andrew Johnson became president following the assassination of Lincoln, and he shared Lincoln's goals for the future; but Johnson was politically weaker than Lincoln and the abolitionists began to push to achieve their goals. With the exception of Tennessee, Johnson's home state, the South was divided into military districts, with state and local governments operating under the supervision of army officers. These governments had to approve equality as defined in the Fourteenth and Fifteenth Amendments in order to have military control lifted. As this program began to be enforced, the Klan concept started to spread.

The Klan remained a local organization, not spreading much beyond Pulaski, until 1867 when a move by the Tennessee General

Assembly changed politics in the state forever. At the end of the war the state legislature of Tennessee denied former Confederates the right to vote. This meant members of state and local governments were elected by the minority of citizens who had been loyal to the United States during the war—the backbone of the Republican party—and by people who had moved to Tennessee since the end of the conflict. The latter were often derisively called "carpetbaggers" since they were said to carry all they owned in a cheap bag made of carpet scraps and had come south solely to take advantage of the chaotic economic conditions.

Seeking to increase their voting strength, the Republican-dominated General Assembly granted the right to vote to African-American males twenty-one years of age and older. This was before the Fourteenth Amendment to the US Constitution was introduced and made Tennessee the fifth state in the nation to grant the franchise to people of color. Allowing African Americans to vote while white ex-Confederates could not vote brought about a strong reaction.

Such a move was a social revolution. The war had effectively ended slavery, and the passage of the Thirteenth Amendment had made that a legal reality. Five million white Southerners suddenly found themselves surrounded by nearly four million black Southerners whose status had changed from "slave" to "free." Now the Tennessee General Assembly, and soon the United States Congress, was proposing that these former slaves be not only free but also equal.

In 1867 the Ku Klux Klan realized it could be active in opposing a state government dominated by Unionists and African

Americans by undertaking a campaign of intimidation to keep Republican voters from the polls. The Klan already had an organizational structure and was accustomed to wearing disguises; now it had a new and sinister purpose. The first recorded act of violence took place in December 1867 and in a short time the various "dens" of the Klan proved that if threats did not keep Republicans, black and white, from registering to vote and from going to the polls, the Klan was quite willing to use beatings and murder to achieve their ends.

The goal of opposing the Reconstruction government was popular among the disenfranchised whites, and the number of Klan members grew. When the Congress of the United States began to discuss the passage of the Fourteenth and Fifteenth Amendments to the Constitution, the resistance to equality spread across the South. Nationally circulated newspapers gave a good deal of coverage to these acts of violence, and this publicity helped spread the notion of the Klan over a wide area.

With growth came a realization that better organization was needed, a conclusion not surprising among a group of men who were veterans of the Confederate armies. In April 1867 conservative Democrats from across Tennessee held a meeting in Nashville for the purpose of finding legal ways of opposing the Republican plan of Reconstruction. At this point tradition replaces history for an account of what took place. Tradition and folklore has it that some of the conservatives, who were associated with the Klan or who had heard about the Klan, met in a hotel room and decided to draw up a constitution, which they called the "Precept," to guide the actions of the Klan. They decided to select an overall leader, called the "Grand Wizard," to lead the group. Former Confederate general Nathan Bedford Forrest was unanimously selected as the first Grand Wizard. Although this story has been repeated in many books about the Klan and has come to be widely believed, there is no conclusive historical proof to substantiate it.

What is a matter of historical fact is that the Precept was printed at the office of the local newspaper in Pulaski and that dens began to crop up in other parts of Tennessee, northern Mississippi, Alabama, and Georgia.

The Klan seems to have remained limited to a relatively small geographical area, but other people had similar ideas at about the same time. As opposition to the Fourteenth and Fifteenth Amendments spread, groups similar to the Klan, but not affiliated with it, arose. In western Tennessee and in Arkansas a group called the "Palefaces" began a campaign of night-riding and intimidation; in Louisiana and along the Gulf Coast there existed the "Knights of the White Camellia"; and in the Carolinas groups engaged in similar activities called themselves the "Red-shirts." The Klan was not the only group opposing Reconstruction governments and advocating for a return to the political situation that had existed before the Civil War. This means there was not a single, monolithic, Southern organization led by a single person whose members wore white robes and terrorized both African Americans and white Republicans.

There were many such groups, but they were not connected. In addition to the larger, somewhat organized groups were dozens—perhaps hundreds—of groups of two or three or a half-dozen men who would gather for a single night to intimidate, or kill, a person in their community they thought led the local Reconstruction forces. Such groups might commit a single act of violence and then never take such action again.

By 1868 there were many groups of white men in many diverse communities that shared the goal of frustrating the implementation of Reconstruction policies, but they did not know about each other nor did they communicate with each other. The circumstances that motivated these local groups to use violence were unique to the locations where they occurred, and were not coordinated by some mysterious central figure who exercised absolute authority or command to achieve a single goal.

Although these groups shared the common purpose of resisting Reconstruction, they were not united and some of them were quite short-lived. Together, they created chaos in some areas and contributed to the failure of Reconstruction. In areas that had a large African-American population which had some protection by US or state forces, the Klan was not effective. Parts of Southern states that had a significant Unionist population also repressed Klan activities. In Nashville it was estimated that the local den had only fifty members and they were opposed by the city police force. But in rural areas where there was no protection from anti-Klan government forces, the lives and well-being of those who supported Reconstruction were very much at risk. This risk was shared by all those who supported the Republican Party, white as well as black, because the goal of the Klan was to put conservative Democrats back in power while also making sure African Americans provided a ready source of low-wage labor.From 1868 to 1870 violence against Republicans, black and white, became frequent and widespread.

Newly elected president Ulysses S. Grant asked Congress to investigate the situation and the result was the passage in 1870 of a bill known as the "Klan Act," which was designed to discover the leaders of the violence and punish them. A congressional investigating committee subpoenaed, among others, Nathan Bedford Forrest, who was widely suspected of being involved with the Klan. However, after two days of testimony, the congressional committee not only absolved Forrest of any involvement with the Klan, but also congratulated him on his open opposition to the organization. Under the Klan Act, federal authorities did indict about 9,000 individuals for engaging in violence, but only a fraction of this number was convicted and sent to prison. None of those convicted were leaders of large groups; they were all involved only with small, local groups that had used violence to oppose the goals of Reconstruction.

Not widely known is the fact that similar vigilante groups existed in the North during the Reconstruction era. While few African Americans lived in Northern states, those who did were often not welcome and the majority of the white population did not want to see more African Americans moving in, as they were seen as willing to work for lower wages. When the Fifteenth Amendment guaranteeing due process under the law was sent to the states for ratification, New York, Ohio, New Jersey, Delaware, Nebraska, and California all voted against approving the amendment. Local groups in these states that sometimes used a variation of the name "Ku Klux" reinforced the message sent by the rejection of the Fifteenth Amendment.

These night-riding anti-Reconstruction groups did not all exist at the same time. Some were organized after the Klan appeared in Tennessee and some disappeared sooner than others, as local conditions changed. In Tennessee, the birthplace of violent resistance to Reconstruction, the Klan became active in mid-1867 and disbanded in the spring of 1869. The reason for the disappearance of the Klan in Tennessee was political. The newly elected Republican governor, DeWitt Clinton Senter, recognized that it was impossible to govern the state with a majority of the property owners and taxpayers—the ex-Confederates—barred from voting. Governor Senter convinced the General Assembly to pass a bill allowing this group to vote. Since there would now be a majority of white conservative Democrats at the polls, there was no reason to resort to violence to oppose the Republican Party.

The same process was followed in state after state until, by 1876, only Florida and South Carolina still had Republican-dominated state governments. In the presidential election of 1876 the Republican candidate for president, Rutherford B. Hayes, promised to end all attempts to enforce the civil rights guarantees of the Fourteenth and Fifteenth Amendments to the US Constitution if these states would cast their electoral votes for him. With that bargain Reconstruction was over and the Klan disappeared. Although organizations calling themselves the Klan reappeared in the 1920s and still exist today, they have no historical connection to the Reconstruction-era group.

The Ku Klux Klan presents us with a sinister, elusive mystery. There was indeed a group that used fantastic names for its officers, its members did wear disguises, and the group did use violence to intimidate those who wanted to develop the ideas of political and social racial equality. But there never was a single, monolithic organization commanded by a single individual that covered the entire South and was the center of opposition to Reconstruction goals. Why, then, do most people have such an exaggerated concept of what the Klan was?

Carrying out a social revolution by establishing a society reflecting racial equality was a task that proved impossible to complete in the nineteenth century. Many leading national political figures had invested a great deal of influence in working for this goal, and it was not easy to admit that a collection of informal, poorly organized, unrelated local groups could frustrate the power of the United States and its army, which had just won the Civil War. William G. Brownlow, wartime Union governor of Tennessee; Horace Greeley, prominent newspaperman; and Benjamin Butler, a Union general and influential politician, all argued dramatically and at length that the Klan had to be a vast conspiracy in order to frustrate the might of government. Such arguments from these and other men helped create the belief that the Klan was something it was not. In sensational fashion the Klan was depicted as a gigantic political conspiracy.

Newspaper reporters also contributed to the false image of the Klan. Many of the reports about Klan violence were written at long distance; that is, the people writing the articles never interviewed primary sources, but collected snippets of news from whatever sources they could find and then wrote accounts of what they perceived to have happened. The violence about which they wrote was real, but their conclusions about its source were often imaginary. A news report that an unknown group of men in a small village in an obscure part of some Southern state had committed an act of violence against a Republican political activist or office holder was not likely to draw much attention. There was a strong temptation, to which reporters often succumbed, to write that the atrocity had been committed by the Klan and to include the fantastic, weird titles that the group was known to use. Instead of "night-riders," "vigilantes," or "persons unknown" being the guilty party, all such violent actions were blamed on "the Klan." Reading that the Ku Klux Klan was everywhere, the public came to believe that the Klan was universal across the South.

"Blame the Klan" was also a diversion used by the groups that had actually been involved in lawlessness. If there was a den of the Klan in the area, its existence would be known, so if there was an act of violence but no local den, then it could be argued that a group of men from outside the community must have come into the area and done the deed. Unless the local sheriff was sure of local support or had the backing of state and federal officials, such an idea made a convenient excuse for not looking very hard for the perpetrators.

The Ku Klux Klan has come to hold a ghostly, mysterious, elusive place in the history and culture of the United States. Its origins are not shrouded in as much mystery as is often assumed. In fact, one of the founders of the Klan, John C. Lester, wrote a book describing the origin and disbanding of the organization, which is still in print. But myth is often more interesting than history and folklore is recounted more often than history is read, so the mystery and myths surrounding the Klan live on.

Note: As World War I was ending, prejudices toward immigrants, Catholics, and Jews, as well as racial prejudices, produced another group that borrowed the name Ku Klux Klan. This group spread nationwide and on August 8, 1925, more than 30,000 of its members marched down Pennsylvania Avenue in Washington, DC. This group dressed in the white robes and tall conical hats that have become a part of the popular image of the Klan.

The Department of Justice says that at present (2018) there are dozens of organizations that use some variation of the name, with all these groups combined having a membership of perhaps 8,000.

BIBLIOGRAPHY

Bishop, Jim. *The Day Lincoln Was Shot.* New York: Harper and Brothers, 1955.

Brown, Kent Masterson. *Cushing of Gettysburg: The Story of a Union Artillery Commander.* Lexington: University Press of Kentucky, 1993.

Cadwallader, Sylvanus. *Three Years with Grant.* Edited by Benjamin P. Thomas. New York: Alfred A. Knopf, 1955.

Cummings, Charles M. *Yankee Quaker, Confederate General: The Curious Career of Bushrod Rust Johnson.* Columbus, OH: The General's Books, 1971.

Cussler, Clive, and Craig Dirgo. *The Sea Hunters II.* New York: Simon and Schuster, 1996.

Davis, William C. *Duel between the First Ironclads.* New York: Doubleday & Company, 1975.

Douglas, Henry Kyd. *I Rode with Stonewall.* Chapel Hill: University of North Carolina Press, 1940.

Foner, Eric. *Reconstruction: America's Unfinished Revolution, 1863–1877.* Updated edition. New York: Harper Perennial, 2014.

Henry, Robert Selph. *"First with the Most" Forrest.* Jackson, TN: McCowat-Mercer Press, 1969. First published 1949.

Hicks, Bian, and Schuyler Kropf. *Raising the Hunley.* New York: Ballentine Books, 2002.

Hurst, Jack. *Nathan Bedford Forrest: A Biography.* New York: Alfred A. Knopf, 1993.

Johnson, Michael P., and James L. Roark. *Black Masters: A Free Family of Color in the Old South.* New York: W. W. Norton and Co., 1984.

Klein, Michael J. *The Baltimore Plot.* Yardley, PA: Westholme Publishing, 2008.

Koger, Larry. *Black Slaveowners.* Columbia: University of South Carolina Press, 1985.

Lester, J. C. and D. L. Wilson. *Ku Klux Klan: Its Origin, Growth, and Disbandment.* New York and Washington: Neale Publishing Company, 1905. Reprint by Nabu Public Domain Reprints, printed on demand.

Moore, Frank. *Women of the War: Their Heroism and Self-Sacrifice.* Hartford, CT: S. S. Scranton & Co., 1867. Paperback edition 2004.

Morton, John Watson. *The Artillery of Nathan Bedford Forrest's Cavalry.* Marietta, GA: R. Bemis Publishing Company, 1995. First published 1909.

Parsons, Elaine Frantz. *Ku-Klux: The Birth of the Klan During Reconstruction*. Chapel Hill: University of North Carolina Press, 2015.

Pember, Phoebe Yates. *A Southern Woman's Story*. St. Simons Island, GA: Mockingbird Books, 1974.

Poole, Robert M. *On Hallowed Ground: The Story of Arlington National Cemetery*. New York: Walker & Company, 2009.

Robertson, James I. *Stonewall Jackson: The Man, the Soldier, the Legend*. New York: Simon & Schuster Macmillan, 1997.

Rosen, Robert. *The Jewish Confederates*. Columbia: University of South Carolina Press, 2000.

Simon, Winchester. *The Professor and the Madman*. New York: Harper Collins, 1998.

Simpson, Brooks D. *Ulysses S. Grant: Triumph over Adversity, 1822–1865*. New York: Houghton Mifflin Co., 2000.

Stern, Philip Van Doren. *The Man Who Killed Lincoln: The Story of John Wilkes Booth and His Part in the Assassination*. New York: Random House, 1939.

Taylor, Richard. *Destruction and Reconstruction*. New York: D. Appleton, 1879.

Trudeau, Noah Andre. *Out of the Storm: The End of the Civil War, April–June, 1865*. Boston: Little, Brown and Company, 1994.

Wilbur, C. Keith. *Civil War Medicine, 1861–1865*. Guilford, CT: Globe Pequot Press, 1998.

Wyeth, John Allan. *That Devil Forrest.* Baton Rouge: Louisiana State University Press, 1989. First published 1899.

Young, Mel. *Last Order of the Lost Cause.* Lanham, MD: University Press of America, 1995.

www.abrahamlincolnsclassroom.org

www.civilwarhome.com/medicinehistory.html

www.frenchcreoles.com

www.hunley.org

www.JSOnline.com/news/waukesha/88882607.html; "Civil War Hero from Delafield in Line for Medal of Honor"

www.marinersmuseum.org

www.numa.net/2011/10/hunley-resurfaces/; "Hunley Resurfaces"

www.pddoc.com/skedaddle/articles/1861_assassination_plot .htm; "The Baltimore Plot to Assassinate Abraham Lincoln"

INDEX

About the Author

Michael R. Bradley received a PhD from Vanderbilt University in 1971. He taught US history at Motlow College in Lynchburg, Tennessee, until 2006. He is the author of several Civil War books, including *It Happened in the Civil War* (Globe Pequot Press), *Tullahoma: The 1863 Campaign, With Blood and Fire: Behind Union Lines in Middle Tennessee,* and *The Escort and Staff of Nathan Bedford Forrest.*